Frederick Buechner 101

Essays, Excerpts,
Sermons and Friends

Choreographed by Anne Lamott

Cambridge, MA

Table of Contents

Welcome
by Anne Lamott

I have been foisting Frederick Buechner's books at religious friends for thirty years now. I think I can be a pest in my insistence that anyone interested in God, grace, meaning, and truth needs to immerse his or herself in his memoirs, essays, novels, and sermons. (He is sort of annoyingly prolific, putting the rest of us writers to shame, with 36 published books so far, some of them bestsellers, and one (*Godric*) a finalist for the Pulitzer Prize. But he writes about the most important issues of our lives, with such wisdom, understanding and wit, that one forgives him all over again for his genius.)

I thrust him into people's unsuspecting hands; *Telling Secrets*, or *Godric*, or *The Sacred Journey*, and tell them, "You have got to read this."

They take a stab at his name: "Boooookner, rhymes with Kookner? Broochner?"

No, Beekner, Frederick Buechner, the person I consider America's most important living theologian, that most amazing mixed grill of gentle intelligence: a brilliant, lovely religious thinker with a great sense of humor, and a first class writer.

Someone first foisted him into my hands in a derided sermon, when I was still teaching writing, at the very end of my drinking, which is to say, the end of my rope.

I have read this paragraph from *Whistling in the Dark* to every single class I have ever taught. I think it is my single favorite passage in his books:

> "From the simplest lyric to the most complex novel and densest drama, literature is asking us to pay attention. Pay attention to the frog. Pay attention to the west wind. Pay attention to the boy on the raft, the lady in the tower, the old man on the train. In sum, pay attention to the world and all that dwells therein and thereby learn at last to pay attention to yourself and all that dwells therein."

Which is God, and which is the kingdom, right? Even typing it up now, I am blown away by how Buechner manages to be both plain and majestic at the same time.

Two years later, when I got sober, someone gave me another of his books, *The Alphabet of Grace*. I read *Alphabet* over and over, like I read C.S. Lewis's *Mere Christianity*. No one has brought me closer to God than these two men.

Both of them were great preachers and teachers, and writers. Both would have been famous as only theologians, or only writers, but they were both. Be still my heart.

The way Buechner writes about the natural word can bring tears to my eyes, because he sees and conveys both the visible and divine beauty in the wild strawberry and the stars, a chickadee and sweet human behavior. His sense of humanity informs my own now, of our dark confusion and radiant hopes, our selfish strivings, and gorgeous tenderness, our ruin and resurrection. He has been, like all great mentors, marbled into me, even as he has stimulated and goaded me into deeper self-discovery.

A few years later, when I saw some words of his used as the epigraph in the marvelous *Prayers for Owen Meany*, written by one of his early students, John Irving, my heart leapt, as if a friend had hit the big time:

> "Not the least of my problems is that I can hardly even imagine what kind of an experience a genuine, self-authenticating religious experience would be. Without somehow destroying me in the process, how could God reveal himself in a way that would leave no room for doubt? If there was no room for doubt, there would be no room for me."

Buechner writes of the truth, both of the Gospel, and of his own damaged family, and of our truth, sight unseen—we've never met—in a way that is so precise, revelatory and profound, that it makes me experience an awakening to spiritual reality all over again, each time. He writes about the joy and grief and mystery and confusion of each human life, his faith journey, his family, the existence of God in the most unlikely places, ie. right in front of your damn nose, in the meadow, in the baby, in the sky, in the apple tree. He writes about listening, to your own heart, to the rhythms and narrative of your own life.

And he understands how fickle and confused we are better than any preacher I've ever heard. Forget what I said about the above passage being my favorite: listen to this one, from his novel *The Return of Ansel Gibbs*:

> "If you tell me Christian commitment is a kind of thing that has happened to you once and for all like some kind of spiritual plastic surgery, I say go to, go to, you're either pulling the wool over your own eyes or trying to pull it over mine. Every morning you should wake up in your bed and ask yourself: "Can I believe it all again today?" No, better still, don't ask it till after you've read *The New York Times*, till after you've studied that daily record of the world's brokenness and corruption, which should always stand side by side with your Bible. Then ask yourself if you can believe in the Gospel of Jesus Christ again for that particular day. If your answer's always Yes, then you probably don't know what believing means. At least five times out of ten the answer should be No because the No is as important as the Yes, maybe more so. The No is what proves you're human in case you should ever doubt it. And then if some morning the answer happens to be really Yes, it should be a Yes that's choked with confession and tears and...great laughter."

How can someone, writing about grace, or angels, or human stupidity, make me laugh out loud?

He has the most beautiful humility.

He is so recognizable, as a wise uncle, who does not talk down to you, who does not make you feel clueless for not understanding the great themes of our lives, but who gently, in language that is both gorgeous and plain, throws on the lights for you, accompanies you on your own journey.

In closing, I have to add that Buechner writes about forgiveness like no one else can. He makes me feel that he would love and understand me, exactly as I am, right now, which believe me, is sort of a quirky mess. He manages to convince me that Jesus would, too. He helps me with the hardest work of all, self-love, and forgiveness of self.

I have a file on my desk called Buechner / Forgiveness, that contains these words, originally from *Wishful Thinking* and later found in *Beyond Words*. Better sit down; it's long. And in fact, forget what I said about the Ansel Gibbs one. THESE may in fact be my favorite passages of all. If you don't love it, we will happily refund your misery:

> "To forgive somebody is to say one way or another, 'You have done something unspeakable, and by all rights I should call it quits between us. Both my pride and my principles demand no less. However, although I make no guarantees that I will be able to forget what you've done, and though we may both carry the scars for life, I refuse to let it stand between us. I still want you for my friend.'

To accept forgiveness means to admit that you've done something unspeakable that needs to be forgiven, and thus both parties must swallow the same thing: their pride.

This seems to explain what Jesus means when he says to God, 'Forgive us our trespasses as we forgive those who trespass against us.' Jesus is not saying that God's forgiveness is conditional upon our forgiving others. In the first place, forgiveness that's conditional isn't really forgiveness at all, just fair warning; and in the second place, our unforgivingness is among those things about us that we need to have God forgive us most. What Jesus apparently is saying is that the pride that keeps us from forgiving is the same pride that keeps us from accepting forgiveness, and will God please help us do something about it.

When somebody you've wronged forgives you, you're spared the dull and self-diminishing throb of a guilty conscience.

When you forgive somebody who has wronged you, you're spared the dismal corrosion of bitterness and wounded pride.

For both parties, forgiveness means the freedom again to be at peace inside their own skins and to be glad in each other's presence."

I wish someone would call me every morning and ask that I re-read this. I wish when I was in trouble, even more lost than usual, a friend would just remind me to read his commencement address ("The Road Goes On" found in this book). It instantly restores me to sanity, a sense of purpose, and joy.

Frederick and I have never met, but he is my dear older brother, and I know I am his dear baby sister, and in this compilation of his words, and words about him, we hope to introduce you to his beautiful brotherhood, too.

Introduction
to Buechner

Brian McLaren's Foreword
to *Secrets in the Dark*

P eople who are afflicted with the twin passions of preaching and writing will probably agree that each benefits the other. For example, in writing, when you slowly and painstakingly fold a clever crease in syntax, when you layer and lean parallelisms one upon another just so, when you learn to signal your logical connections with sturdy connecting words like indeed, however; and for example, you practice skills that are likely to sneak out when you preach-to your surprise and your hearers' delight.

And similarly, preaching can't help but teach you something about writing. You learn to feel the rhythm of a sentence. You imagine actual readers encountering your words in real time. You learn to simplify, which is harder than it looks. You learn to write in a whisper, maybe; to romance your readers with a tiny scrap of punctuation-just as you might do with a gesture or sigh when you preach. In fact, if you practice enough writing and preaching, and if you are blessed with extraordinary natural aptitudes from the start, you have the chance of spiraling into greatness. You may even excel beyond that and become a Frederick Buechner.

I have no desire to analyze what makes Buechner's writing and preaching so extraordinary. Neither do I want to account for Bob Dylan's raspy mystique, the peculiar beauty of a rainbow trout in a riffle, or a thunderstorm's magnetic terror. I simply want to enjoy them. They all knock me out of analysis and smack me clear into pleasure and awe. So, in Buechner's case, please spare me the burden of analysis and permit me the pleasure of observation - the kind of thing you might say to your spouse or best friend when you have a favorite CD playing on a long drive, or are on vacation when the afternoon sky grows angry dark, or are cooling your feet in a creek: Did you catch that line in "Every Grain of Sand"? Whoa-did you see that flash of lightning? Look, there, in that still patch stream from that boulder-see it?

If we were sitting on a park bench together, reading these sermons of Fred Buechner, I'd keep interrupting you with similarly annoying questions.

Do you see why, in "The Two Stories," for example, his narrative approach is a far cry from telling little anecdotes to illustrate points? In "The Truth of Stories," did you catch how the story is not like an orange rind, but that it is itself the point, or at least the thing that points beyond itself to something more?

Did you catch how, in the shepherd's monologue in "The Birth," Buechner does a kind of reverse on Sartre's Roquentin in La Nausee? Remember how Sartre's character, sitting on a park bench and staring at a root protruding beneath his feet, saw through existence into the nihil the absence of essence - and the vision made him retch? See how Buechner's shepherd sees into (not through) existence and goes ecstatic by encountering glory?

And when Buechner shares one of his own visions of glory - entering New York, in "The Kingdom of God," or at Sea World (of all places) watching killer whales, in "The Great Dance"- didn't you almost feel it too?

And did you realize that you had in fact seen it, a thousand times, but only at that moment of reading did you realize you had seen it?

Will you ever be able to read the Noah's ark story the same way again after reading "A Sprig of Hope"? And did you notice how, against the darkness and stench of that not-really-for-children story, Buechner manages to talk sincerely about peace and love? What could be more clichéd than that?

Yet he never sounds the slightest bit corny. Why is his modest little title so much bigger and robust than "The Depth of the Flood" or "Noah's Escape from Despair" would have been?

Did you notice the way Buechner guides us beyond the things fundamentalists and liberals always argue about-in "Come and See," for example, or in "The Seeing Heart"? If you're a preacher yourself did you notice that many of the best sermons are the shortest ones, and did you feel embarrassed and stupid for being so long-winded so often, as I did? Have you ever read a better introduction to the Bible than "The Good Book as a Good Book" or a better overview of a book of the Bible than "Paul Sends His Love"?

What? You'd like me to shut up? You'd like me to stop telling you what I noticed and enjoyed in these sermons, so you can embark on your own reading—and notice things for yourself? No worries and no offense taken. I understand exactly how you feel.

A new generation of preachers is coming up, and I can't think of anyone more enjoyable and exemplary for them to read than Buechner. They need to observe his art in creating an old woman with thick glasses, eating popcorn at the movies, or a fat man in a pickup, complete with gun rack and Jesus Loves You sticker (in "The Church"). They need to reflect on how these characters - sketched so minimally - do something that elegant points or abstractions never could have, especially when Buechner brings them back later in the sermon, adding one devastating detail to each.

The next generation of preachers will learn something precious from Buechner in this and a dozen other ways, not, we hope, so they can analyze it or talk about it, but so they can actually catch something of his art, his eye, his heart, so they unconsciously, accidentally, might trade in a few of their points and abstractions for a teenage girl with acne, smoking a cigarette, or the young bride in high heels wobbling down the aisle on her father's arm.

This new generation of preachers will have a natural affinity to Buechner because he, unlike a popular painter known as the "painter of light," never paints light without shadows. Buechner's faith carries freight because it has not come easy; it dances and sometimes street-fights with doubt. He calls himself "this skeptical old believer, this believing old skeptic." The young preachers I know are tired to death of easy answers and simple steps and cozy scenes with serene porch lights and perfect picket fences. They don't live in that world. They live in a world of thick glasses, gun racks, acne, and cancer. And so do the people they preach to. Which is the world Buechner celebrates in his sermons. This world is the very one in which he keeps bumping into the living God, or vice versa. Which is why young preachers need to read these sermons.

In "Faith and Fiction," Buechner describes writing as whistling in the dark. And, no doubt, he'd say preaching is something like that too: maybe in part both are attempts to convince yourself "that dark is not all there is." But surely both are more: disciplines-like Godric's bath in frigid water-to remind yourself that beyond all dark is a shining river of light, and "all the death that ever was, set next to life, would scarcely fill a cup."

"Dear Mr. Buechner, you rearranged the air"
A Tribute to Frederick Buechner

By Barbara Brown Taylor

I had been out of seminary for not quite a year in February of 1977—not long enough to decide what to do, either with my divinity degree or with the rest of my life. I was typing other people's letters for a living, helping out with the church youth group on weekends. I was single then, so there were also men (who shall remain forever nameless), but my great love affair in those days was with language: with words, images, metaphors, and meanings. I had so much to say that I thought I could not say in church—fleshy things that were not religiously correct, melancholy things that seemed to betray the good news. So I wrote tortured short stories instead. I wrote poems so bad that they made my teeth ache.

When I received a flyer from Yale Divinity School announcing the Beecher Lectures in Preaching, I thought maybe that was the kick in the pants I needed. I did not know the lecturer, but that hardly mattered. I wanted to hear the clock on the quadrangle strike the hours again, see my old friends, maybe grab a beer at Archie's bar down on Willow Street. Still, I was paying attention when the dean introduced Frederick Buechner, the Beecher Lecturer for 1977, whose lectures were entitled "Telling the Truth: The Gospel as Tragedy, Comedy and Fairy Tale."

Great title, I thought, as the elegant man stepped into the pulpit. When he opened his mouth, I was struck first by the voice: restrained but insistent, as if he had something important to tell that he would not yell to make heard. Then the sentence structure: odd and looping; beguiling the ear. Before I knew it, he was conjuring up the living presence of Henry Ward Beecher, his predecessor by more than a century, the *first* Beecher Lecturer in 1872.

Beecher had had a bad night, Buechner told us. With less than an hour to go before his first lecture, the famous preacher still had not decided what to say. Lathering his face to shave, Beecher was struck by sudden inspiration, dropped his razor, and dashed off to find a pencil with the suds still on his chin. When he returned to the mirror to finish shaving, he was so shaky that he nicked himself and drew blood.

"And well the old pulpiteer might have cut himself with his razor," Buechner said, "because part of the inner world that his lecture came from, among the clouds that it suddenly dawned on him out of, was the deep trouble he was in or the deep trouble that was in him. The gossip about his relationship with the wife of one of his parishioners had left the whispering stage and was beginning to appear more or less directly in print… A public trial for adultery was not far off. It was not just his reputation and career that were in danger but in some measure the church itself—everything he believed in and stood for and had come to Yale to talk about."

Less than five minutes in, Buechner had already given me blood, a bad night's sleep, self-doubt, and an illicit affair—*Mon Dieu!*—the ragged private truths of a well-pressed public preacher. Were we really going to speak of such things in church? I had never heard anyone go so directly to the heart of the matter, nor use language to get there so movingly. As the lecture continued, I was slain in the spirit, though still propped up in my pew. I was known through and through, though my name was never called. Dear Mr. Buechner, you rearranged the air.

Three days later, when you finished your last lecture, I felt as if a major artery in my heart were being clamped off. I could have listened to you forever. But even after you stopped talking, your voice stayed alive in my ear. To this day, you have remained one of my best angels, and not just mine but all of ours, who—week after week—trust that our nicked and ragged selves, however hard we try to press them, will somehow serve to bring God's truth to life.

From you, I have learned that it is only when I give my full attention to what it means to be human that I am granted a glimpse of what it means to be divine.

From you, I have learned that the only limit to the revelation going on all around me is my willingness to turn aside and look.

From you, I have learned that language itself is revelatory, with power to ignite hearts, move mountains, and save lives.

From you, I have learned that the good news is not the cheerful news but the dismantling news of what it is like both to love and to betray the Holy One who has given me life, only to hear the saving question asked anew, for the umpteenth time, "You, you child of mine, Do you love me?"

Thank you, Frederick Buechner, for the time you have spent looking in the mirror so that we might see ourselves more clearly. Thank you for telling the truth, both about yourself and about the gospel, so that we might tell it too. Thanks even for nicking yourself, so that you could write for us in blood instead of ballpoint pen. We can tell the difference, and we are in your debt.

Barbara Brown Taylor
Washington National Cathedral
April 5, 2006

The Road Goes On

The following is Buechner's commencement address at the Union Theological Seminary in Richmond, VA; published in "A Room Called Remember"

JOHN 14:6
Jesus said to him, "I am the way,
and the truth, and the life."

Here I am, and there you are. That is the crux of it. Here I am, the stranger in your midst. There you are, who are the midst, who are the graduating class, who are friends and classmates and sweethearts of each other, who have brought your friends and families with you and yet who are—all of you, even those of you who have known each other for years and whose hearts are sweetest—as much strangers to each other in many ways as I am a stranger to you all. Because how can we be other than strangers when at those rare moments of our lives when we stop hiding from each other and try instead passionately and profoundly to make ourselves known to each other, we find this is precisely what we cannot do?

And yet in another sense we are none of us strangers. Not even I. Not even you. Because how can we be strangers when, for all these years, we have ridden on the back of this same rogue planet, when we have awakened to the same sun and dreamed the same dreams under the same moon? How can we be strangers when we are all of us in the same interior war and do battle with the same interior enemy, which is most of the time ourselves? How can we be strangers when we laugh and cry at the same things and have the same bad habits and occasionally astonish ourselves and everybody else by performing the same uncharacteristic deeds of disinterested kindness and love?

We are strangers and we are not strangers. The question is: Can anything that really matters humanly pass between us? The question is: Can God in his grace and power speak anything that matters ultimately through the likes of me to the likes of you? And I am saying all these things not just to point up the difficulties of delivering a commencement address like this. Who cares about that? I am saying them because in the place where I am standing now, or places just as improbable, you will be standing soon enough as your turn comes. And much of what this day means is that your turn has come at last.

As ministers, preachers, prophets, pastors, teachers, administrators and who knows what-all else of churches, you will be leaving this lovely place for places as lovely or lovelier yet or not lovely at all where you will take your turn at doing essentially what I am here to do now, which is one way or another to be, however inadequately, a servant of Christ. I wouldn't have dreamed of packing my bag and driving a thousand miles except for Christ. I wouldn't have the brass to stand here before you now if the only words I had to speak were the ones I had cooked up for the occasion. I am here, Heaven help me, because I believe that from time to time we are given something of Christ's word to speak if we can only get it out through the clutter and cleverness of our own speaking. And I believe that in the last analysis, whatever other reasons you have for being here yourselves, Christ is at the bottom of why you are here too. We are all here because of him. This is his day as much as, if not more than, it is ours. If it weren't for him, we would be somewhere else.

Our business is to be the hands and feet and mouths of one who has no other hands or feet or mouth except our own. It gives you pause. Our business is to work for Christ as surely as men and women in other trades work for presidents of banks or managers of stores or principals of high schools. Whatever salaries you draw, whatever fringe benefits you receive, your recompense will be ultimately from Christ, and a strange and unforeseeable and wondrous recompense I suspect it will be, and with many a string attached to it too. Whatever real success you have will be measured finally in terms of how well you please not anyone else in all this world—including your presbyteries, your bishops, your congregations—but only Christ, and I suspect that the successes that please him best are very often the ones that we don't even notice. Christ is the one who will be hurt, finally, by your failures. If you are to be healed, comforted, sustained during the dark times that will come to you as surely as they have come to everyone else who has ever gone into this strange trade, Christ will be the one to sustain you because there is no one else in all this world with love enough and power enough to do so. It is worth thinking about.

Christ is our employer as surely as the general contractor is the carpenter's employer, only the chances are that this side of Paradise we will never see his face except mirrored darkly in dreams and shadows, if we're lucky, and in each other's faces. He is our general, but the chances are that this side of Paradise we will never hear his voice except in the depth of our own inner silence and in each other's voices. He is our shepherd, but the chances are we will never feel his touch except as we are touched by the joy and pain and holiness of our own life and each other's lives. He is our pilot, our guide, our true, fast, final friend and judge, but often when we need him most, he seems farthest away because he will always have gone on ahead, leaving only the faint print of his feet on the path to follow. And the world blows leaves across the path. And branches fall. And darkness falls. We are, all of us, Mary Magdalene, who reached out to him at the end only to embrace the empty air. We are the ones who stopped for a bite to eat that evening at Emmaus and, as soon as they saw who it was that was sitting there at the table with them, found him vanished from their sight. Abraham, Moses, Gideon, Rahab, Sarah are our brothers and sisters because, like them, we all must live *in faith,* as the great chapter puts it with a staggering honesty that should be a lesson to us all, "not having received what was promised, but having seen it and greeted it from afar," and only from afar. And yet the country we seek and do not truly find, at least not here, not now, the heavenly country and homeland, is there somewhere as surely as our yearning for it is there; and I think that our yearning for it is itself as much apart of the truth of it as our yearning for love or beauty or peace is apart of those truths. And Christ is there with us on our way as surely as the way itself is there that has brought us to this place. It has brought us. We are here. He is with us—that is our faith—but only in unseen ways, as subtle and pervasive as air. As for what it remains for you and me to do, maybe T. S. Eliot says it as poignantly as anybody.

> ... wait without hope
> For hope would be hope of the wrong thing; wait
>   without love
> For love would be love of the wrong thing; there
>   is yet faith
> But the faith and the love and the hope are all in
>   the waiting.
> Wait without thought, for you are not ready for
>   thought:
> So the darkness shall be light, and the stillness the
>   dancing.

It's a queer business that you have chosen or that has chosen you. It's a business that breaks the heart for the sake of the heart. It's a hard and chancy business whose risks are as great even as its rewards. Above all else, perhaps, it is a crazy business. It is a foolish business. It is a crazy and foolish business to work for Christ in a world where most people most of the time don't give a hoot in hell whether you work for him or not. It is crazy and foolish to offer a service that most people most of the time think they need like a hole in the head. As long as there are bones to set and drains to unclog and children to tame and boredom to survive, we need doctors and plumbers and teachers and people who play the musical saw; but when it comes to the business of Christ and his church, how unreal and irrelevant a service that seems even, and at times especially, to the ones who are called to work at it.

"We are fools for Christ's sake," Paul says. You can't put it much more plainly than that. God is foolish too, he says—"the foolishness of God"—just as plainly. God is foolish to choose for his holy work in the world the kind of lamebrains and misfits and nitpickers and holier-than-thous and stuffed shirts and odd ducks and egomaniacs and milquetoasts and closet sensualists as are vividly represented here by you and me this spring evening. God is foolish to send us out to speak hope to a world that slogs along heart-deep in the conviction that from here on out things can only get worse. To speak of realities we cannot see when the realities we see all too well are already more than we can handle. To speak of loving our enemies when we have a hard enough time of it just loving our friends.

To be all things to all people when it's usually all we can do to be anything that matters much to anybody. To proclaim eternal life in a world that is as obsessed with death as a quick browse through *TV Guide* or the newspapers or the drugstore paperbacks make plain enough. God is foolish to send us out on a journey for which there are no sure maps. Such is the foolishness of God.

And yet. The "and yet" of it is our faith, of course. And yet, Paul says, "the foolishness of God is wiser than men," which is to say that in some unsearchable way he may even know what he is doing. Praise him.

If I were braver than I am, I would sing you a song at this point. If you were braver than you are, you might even encourage me to. But let me at least say you a song. It is from *The Lord Of the Rings,* and Bilbo Baggins sings it. It goes like this.

> The road goes ever on and on
> Down from the door where it began.
> Now far ahead the road has gone,
> And I must follow if I can,
> Pursuing it with weary feet,
> Until it joins some larger way,
> Where many paths and errands meet.
> And whither then?
> I cannot say.

"I am the way," Jesus said. I am the road. And in some foolish fashion, we are all on the road that is his, that is he, or such at least is our hope and prayer. That is why we are here at this turning of the road. There is not a single shoe in this place that does not contain a foot of clay, a foot that drags, a foot that stumbles; but on just such feet we all seek to follow that road through a world where there are many other roads to follow, and hardly a one of them that is not more clearly marked and easier to tramp and toward an end more known, more assured, more realizable. But we have picked this road, or been picked by it. "I am the way," he said, "the truth and the life." We have come this far along the *way.* From time to time, when we have our wits about us, when our hearts are in the right place, when nothing more enticing or immediate shows up to distract us, we have glimpsed that *truth*. From time to time when the complex and wearisome and seductive business of living doesn't get in our way, our pulses have quickened and gladdened to the pulse of that *life*. Who knows what the mysteries of our faith mean? Who knows what the Holy Spirit means? Who knows what the Resurrection means? Who knows what he means when he tells us that whenever two or three are gathered together in his name, he will be with them? But what at the very least they seem to mean is that there winds through all we think of as real life a way of life, a way to life, that is so vastly realer still that we cannot think of him, whose way it is, as anything less than vastly alive.

By grace we are on that way. By grace there come unbidden moments when we feel in our bones what it is like to be on that way. Our clay feet drag us to the bedroom of the garrulous old woman, to the alcoholic who for the tenth time has phoned to threaten suicide just as we are sitting down to supper, to the laying of the cornerstone of the new gym to deliver ourselves of a prayer that nobody much listens to, to the Bible study group where nobody has done any studying, to the Xerox machine. We don't want to go. We go in fear of the terrible needs of the ones we go to. We go in fear of our own emptiness from which it is hard to believe that any word or deed of help or hope or healing can come. But we go because it is where his way leads us; and again and again we are blessed by our going in ways we can never anticipate, and our going becomes a blessing to the ones we go to because when we follow his way, we never go entirely alone, and it is always something more than just ourselves and our own emptiness that we bring. Is that true? Is it true in the sense that it is true that there are seven days in a week and that light travels faster than sound? Maybe the final answer that faith can give to that awesome and final question occurs in a letter that Dostoevski wrote to a friend in 1854. "If anyone proved to me that Christ was outside the truth," he wrote, "and it really was so that the truth was outside Christ, then I would prefer to remain with Christ than with the truth."

"The road goes ever on and on," the song says, "down from the door where it began," and for each of us there was a different door, and we all have different tales to tell of where and when and how our journeys began. Perhaps there was no single moment but rather a series of moments that together started us off. For me, there was hearing a drunken blasphemy in a bar. There was a dream where I found myself writing down a name which, though I couldn't remember it when I woke up, I knew was the true and secret name of everything that matters or could ever matter. As I lay on the grass one afternoon thinking that if ever I was going to know the truth in all its fullness, it was going to be then, there was a stirring in the air that made two apple branches strike against each other with a wooden clack, and I suspect that any more of the truth than that would have been the end of me instead of, as it turned out, part of the beginning.

Such moments as those, and others no less foolish, were, together, the door from which the road began for me, and who knows where it began for each of you. But this much at least, I think, would be true for us all: that one way or another the road starts off from passion—a passion for what is holy and hidden, a passion for Christ. It is a little like falling in love, or, to put it more accurately, I suppose, falling in love is a little like it. The breath quickens. Scales fall from the eyes. A world within the world flames up. If you are Simeon Stylites, you spend the rest of your days perched on a flagpole. If you are Saint Francis, you go out and preach to the red-winged blackbirds. If you are Albert Schweitzer, you give up theology and Bach and go to medical school. And if that sort of thing is too rich for your blood, you go to a seminary. You did. I did. And for some of us, it's not all that crazy a thing to do.

It's not such a crazy thing to do because if seminaries don't as a rule turn out saints and heroes, they at least teach you a thing or two. "God has made foolish the wisdom of the world," Paul says, but not until wisdom has served its purpose. Passion is all very well. It is all very well to fall in love. But passion must be grounded, or like lightning without a lightning rod it can blow fuses and burn the house down. Passion must be related not just to the world inside your skin where it is born but to the world outside your skin where it has to learn to walk and talk and act in terms of social justice and human need and politics and nuclear power and God knows what-all else or otherwise become as shadowy and irrelevant as all the other good intentions that the way to hell is paved with. Passion must be harnessed and put to work, and the power that first stirs the heart must become the power that also stirs the hands and feet because it is the places your feet take you to and the work you find for your hands that finally proclaim who you are and who Christ is. Passion without wisdom to give it shape and direction is as empty as wisdom without passion to give it power and purpose. So you sit at the feet of the wise and learn what they have to teach, and our debts to them are so great that, if your experience is like mine, even twenty-five years later you will draw on the depth and breadth of their insights, and their voices will speak in you still, and again and again you will find yourself speaking in their voices. You learn as much as you can from the wise until finally, if you do it right and things break your way, you are wise enough to be yourself, and brave enough to speak with your own voice, and foolish enough, for Christ's sake, to live and serve out of the uniqueness of your own vision of him and out of your own passion.

"And whither then?" the song asks. The world of *The Lord of the Rings* is an enchanted world. It is a shadowy world where life and death are at stake and where things are seldom what they seem. It is a dangerous and beautiful world in which great evil and great good are engaged in a battle where more often than not the odds are heavily in favor of great evil. It is a world where enormous burdens are loaded on small shoulders and where the most fateful issues hang on what are apparently the most homely and insignificant decisions. And thus it is through a world in many ways much like our own that the road winds.

You will be ordained, many of you, or have been already, and if again your experience is anything like mine, you will find, or have found, that something more even than an outlandish new title and an outlandish new set of responsibilities is conferred in that outlandish ceremony. Without wanting to sound unduly fanciful, I think it is fair to say that an extraordinary new adventure begins with ordination, a new stretch of the road, that is unlike any other that you have either experienced or imagined. Your life is no longer your own in the same sense. You are not any more virtuous than you ever were—certainly no new sanctity or wisdom or power suddenly descends—but you are nonetheless "on call" in a new way. You start moving through the world as the declared representative of what people variously see as either the world's oldest and most persistent and superannuated superstition, or the world's wildest and most improbable dream, or the holy, living truth itself. In unexpected ways and at unexpected times people of all sorts, believers and unbelievers alike, make their way to you looking for something that often they themselves can't name any more than you can well name it to them. Often their lives touch yours at the moments when they are most vulnerable, when some great grief or gladness or perplexity has swept away all the usual barriers we erect between each other so that you see them for a little as who they really are, and you yourself are stripped naked by their nakedness.

Strange things happen. Again and again Christ is present not where, as priests, you would be apt to look for him but precisely where you wouldn't have thought to look for him in a thousand years. The great preacher, the sunset, the Mozart Requiem can leave you cold, but the child in the doorway, the rain on the roof, the half-remembered dream, can speak of him and for him with an eloquence that turns your knees to water. The decisions you think are most important turn out not to matter so much after all, but whether or not you mail the letter, the way you say goodbye or decide not to say it, the afternoon you cancel everything and drive out to the beach to watch the tide come in—these are apt to be the moments when souls are won or lost, including quite possibly your own.

You come to places where many paths and errands meet, as the song says, as all our paths meet for a moment here, we friends who are strangers, we strangers who are friends. Great possibilities for good or for ill may come of the meeting, and often it is the leaden casket rather than the golden casket that contains the treasure, and the one who seems to have least to offer turns out to be the one who has most.

"And whither then?" Whither now? "I cannot say," the singer says, nor yet can I. But far ahead the road goes on anyway, and we must follow if we can because it is our road, it is his road, it is the only road that matters when you come right down to it. Let me finally say only this one thing more.

I was sitting by the side of the road one day last fall. It was a dark time in my life. I was full of anxiety, full of fear and uncertainty. The world within seemed as shadowy as the world without. And then, as I sat there, I spotted a car coming down the road toward me with one of those license plates that you can get by paying a little extra with a word on it instead of just numbers and a letter or two. And of all the words the license plate might have had on it, the word that it did have was the word T-R-U-S-T: TRUST. And as it came close enough for me to read, it became suddenly for me a word from on high, and I give it to you here as a word from on high also for you, a kind of graduation present.

The world is full of dark shadows to be sure, both the world without and the world within, and the road we've all set off on is long and hard and often hard to find, but the word is *trust*. Trust the deepest intuitions of your own heart. Trust the source of your own truest gladness. Trust the road. Above all else, trust him. Trust him. Amen.

Buechner's Story

Excerpts from
The Sacred Journey:
A Memoir of Early Days

About ten years ago I gave a set of lectures at Harvard in which I made the observation that all theology, like all fiction, is at its heart autobiography, and that what a theologian is doing essentially is examining as honestly as he can the rough-and-tumble of his own experience with all its ups and downs, its mysteries and loose ends, and expressing in logical, abstract terms the truths about human life and about God that he believes he has found implicit there. More as a novelist than as a theologian, more concretely than abstractly, I determined to try to describe my own life as evocatively and candidly as I could in the hope that such glimmers of theological truth as I believed I had glimpsed in it would shine through my description more or less on their own. It seemed to me then, and seems to me still, that if God speaks to us at all in this world, if God speaks anywhere, it is into our personal lives that he speaks. Someone we love dies, say. Some unforeseen act of kindness or cruelty touches the heart or makes the blood run cold. We fail a friend, or a friend fails us, and we are appalled at the capacity we all of us have for estranging the very people in our lives we need the most. Or maybe nothing extraordinary happens at all-just one day following another, helter-skelter, in the manner of days. We sleep and dream. We wake. We work. We remember and forget. We have fun and are depressed. And into the thick of it, or out of the thick of it, at moments of even the most humdrum of our days, God speaks. But what do I mean by saying that God speaks?

I wrote these words at home on a hot, hazy summer day. On the wall behind me, an old banjo clock was tick-tocking the time away. Outside I could hear the twitter of swallows as they swooped in and out of the eaves of the barn. Every once in a while, in the distance, a rooster crowed, though it was well past sunup. Several rooms away, in another part of the house, two men were doing some carpentry. I could not make out what they were saying, but I was aware of the low rumble of their voices, the muffled sounds of their hammers, and the uneven lengths of silence in between. It was getting on toward noon, and from time to time my stomach growled as it went about its own obscure business which I neither understand nor want to. They were all of them random sounds without any apparent purpose or meaning, and yet as I paused to listen to them, I found myself hearing them with something more than just my ears to the point where they became in some way enormously meaningful. The swallows, the rooster, the workmen, my stomach, all with their elusive rhythms, their harmonies and disharmonies and counterpoint, became, as I listened, the sound of my own life speaking to me. Never had I heard just such a coming together of sounds before, and it is unlikely that I will ever hear them in just the same combination again. Their music was unique and unrepeatable and beyond describing in its freshness. I have no clear idea what the sounds meant or what my life was telling me. What does the song of a swallow mean? What is the muffled sound of a hammer trying to tell? And yet as I listened to those sounds, and listened with something more than just my hearing, I was moved by their inexpressible eloquence and suggestiveness, by the sense I had that they were a music rising up out of the mystery of not just my life, but of life itself. In much the same way, that is what I mean by saying that God speaks into or out of the thick of our days.

He speaks not just through the sounds we hear, of course, but through events in all their complexity and variety, through the harmonies and disharmonies and counterpoint of all that happens. As to the meaning of what he says, there are times that we are apt to think we know. Adolph Hitler dies a suicide in his bunker with the Third Reich going up in flames all around him, and what God is saying about the wages of sin seems clear enough. Or Albert Schweitzer renounces fame as a theologian and musician for a medical mission in Africa, where he ends up even more famous still as one of the great near-saints of Protestantism; and again we are tempted to see God's meaning as clarity itself. But what is God saying through a good man's suicide? What about the danger of the proclaimed saint's becoming a kind of religious prima donna as proud of his own humility as a peacock of its tail? What about sin itself as a means of grace? What about grace, when misappropriated and misunderstood, becoming an occasion for sin? To try to express in even the most insightful and theologically sophisticated terms the meaning of what God speaks through the events of our lives is as precarious a business as to try to express the meaning of the sound of rain on the roof or the spectacle of the setting sun. But I choose to believe that he speaks nonetheless, and the reason that his words are impossible to capture in human language is of course that they are ultimately always incarnate words. They are words fleshed out in the everydayness no less than in the crises of our own experience.

With all this in mind, I entitled those Harvard lectures *The Alphabet of Grace* in order to suggest that life itself can be thought of as an alphabet by which God graciously makes known his presence and purpose and power among us. Like the Hebrew alphabet, the alphabet of grace has no vowels, and in that sense his words to us are always veiled, subtle, cryptic, so that it is left to us to delve their meaning, to fill in the vowels, for ourselves by means of all the faith and imagination we can muster. God speaks to us in such a way, presumably, not because he chooses to be obscure but because, unlike a dictionary word whose meaning is fixed, the meaning of an incarnate word is the meaning it has for the one it is spoken to, the meaning that becomes clear and effective in our lives only when we ferret it out for ourselves. *Heilsgeschichte* is a more theological way of saying the same thing. Deep within history, as it gets itself written down in history books and newspapers, in the letters we write and in the diaries we keep, is sacred history, is God's purpose working itself out in the apparent purposelessness of human history and of our separate histories, is the history, in short, of the saving and losing of souls, including our own. A child is born. A friend is lost or found. Out of nowhere comes a sense of peace or foreboding. We are awakened by a dream. Out of the shadowy street comes a cry for help. We must learn to listen to the cock-crows and hammering and tick-tock of our lives for the holy and elusive word that is spoken to us out of their depths. It is the function of all great preaching, I think, and of all great art, to sharpen our hearing to precisely that end, and it was what I attempted in *The Alphabet of Grace*. I took a single, ordinary day of my life, and in describing the events of it—waking up, dressing, taking the children to school, working, and coming home again—I tried to suggest something of what I thought I had heard God saying.

That was ten years ago. By now my children have mostly grown up and mostly gone. I am not by a long shot entirely grown up myself, but I am ten years' worth of days older than I was then, and lots of things have happened to me, and I have had lots of time to listen to them happening. Also, since I passed the age of fifty, I have taken to looking back on my life as a whole more. I have looked through old letters and dug out old photographs. I have gone through twenty years' worth of old home movies. I have thought about the people I have known and the things that have happened that have, for better or worse, left the deepest mark on me. Like sitting there on the couch listening to the sounds of roosters, swallows, hammers, ticking clock, I have tried to make something out of the hidden alphabet of the years I have lived, to catch, beneath all the random sounds those years have made, a strain at least of their unique music. My interest in the past is not, I think, primarily nostalgic. Like everybody else, I rejoice in much of it and marvel at those moments when, less by effort than by grace, it comes to life again with extraordinary power and immediacy—vanished faces and voices, the feeling of what it was like to fall in love for the first time, of running as a child through the firefly dusk of summer, the fresh linen and cinnamon and servant-swept fragrance of my grandmother's house in Pennsylvania, the taste of snow, the stubbly touch of my father's good-night. But even if it were possible to return to those days, I would never choose to. What quickens my pulse now is the stretch ahead rather than the one behind, and it is mainly for some clue to where I am going that I search through where I have been, for some hint as to who I am becoming or failing to become that I delve into what used to be. I listen back to a time when nothing was much farther from my thoughts than God for an echo of the gutturals and sibilants and vowellessness by which I believe that even then God was addressing me out of my life as he addresses us all. And it is because I believe that, that I think of my life and of the lives of everyone who has ever lived, or will ever live, as not just journeys through time but as sacred journeys.

Ten years ago in those Harvard lectures, I tried to listen to a single day of my life in such a way. What I propose to do now is to try listening to my life as a whole, or at least to certain key moments of the first half of my life thus far, for whatever of meaning, of holiness, of God, there may be in it to hear. My assumption is that the story of anyone of us is in some measure the story of us all. For the reader, I suppose, it is like looking through someone else's photograph album. What holds you, if nothing else, is the possibility that somewhere among all those shots of people you never knew and places you never saw, you may come across something or someone you recognize. In fact—for more curious things have Happened—even in a stranger's album, there is always the possibility that as the pages flip by, on one of them you may even catch a glimpse of yourself. Even if both of those fail, there is still a third possibility which is perhaps the happiest of them all, and that is that once I have put away my album for good, you may in the privacy of the heart take out the album of your own life and search it for the people and places you have loved and learned from yourself, and for those moments in the past—many of them half -forgotten—through which you glimpsed, however dimly and fleetingly, the sacredness of your own journey.

*   *   *

After five years of teaching and the publication of a second novel that fared as badly as the first one had fared well, I gave up my Lawrenceville job and in 1953 went to New York to be a full-time writer, only to discover that I could not write a word. So I decided that maybe I should try to make money instead and went to see a former partner of my uncle about the possibility of going into the advertising business; but he said that although there was plenty of money to be made there, you had to have a very tough hide to survive, and I decided that probably my hide was not tough enough.

So I turned to the CIA, of all things, thinking that if there was going to be another war, I would probably stand a better chance of surviving as a spy than back in the infantry again; but when I was asked by an interviewer in Washington if I would be willing to submit a person to physical torture in order to extract information that many lives might depend on, I decided that I had no stomach for that either, and another road was barred. And somewhere in the process I fell in love again with a girl who did not fall in love with me. It all sounds like a kind of inane farce as I set it down here, with every door I tried to open slammed on my foot, and yet I suppose it was also a kind of pilgrim's progress. I suppose, too, that when you get right down to the flesh and blood of things, the pilgrimage and the farce always go hand in hand because it is a divine comedy that we are all of us involved in after all, not a divine dirge, and when Saint Paul calls us to be fools for Christ, it is not to frock coats and poke bonnets that he is calling us, but to motley and a cap with bells.

Part of the farce was that for the first time in my life that year in New York, I started going to church regularly, and what was farcical about it was not that I went but my reason for going, which was simply that on the same block where I lived there happened to be a church with a preacher I had heard of and that I had nothing all that much better to do with my lonely Sundays. The preacher was a man named George Buttrick, and Sunday after Sunday I went, and sermon after sermon I heard. It was not just his eloquence that kept me coming back, though he was wonderfully eloquent, literate, imaginative, never letting you guess what he was going to come out with next but twitching with surprises up there in the pulpit, his spectacles a-glitter in the lectern light. What drew me more was whatever it was that his sermons came from and whatever it was in me that they touched so deeply. And then there came one particular sermon with one particular phrase in it that does not even appear in a transcript of his words that somebody sent me more than twenty-five years later so I can only assume that he must have dreamed it up at the last minute and ad-libbed it—and on just such foolish, tenuous, holy threads as that, I suppose, hang the destinies of us all. Jesus Christ refused the crown that Satan offered him in the wilderness, Buttrick said, but he is king nonetheless because again and again he is crowned in the heart of the people who believe in him. And that inward coronation takes place, Buttrick said, "among confession, and tears, and great laughter."

It was the phrase *great laughter* that did it, did whatever it was that I believe must have been hiddenly in the doing all the years of my journey up till then. It was not so much that a door opened as that I suddenly found that a door had been open all along which I had only just then stumbled upon. After church, with a great lump still in my throat, I walked up to 84th Street to have Sunday dinner with Grandma Buechner. She sat in her usual chair with the little Philco silent at her side and a glass of sherry in her hand, and when I told her something of what had happened, I could see that she was as much bemused as pleased by what I had said. I have forgotten her words, but the sense of her answer was that she was happy for me that I had found whatever it was that I had found. *Le bon Dieu.* You could never be sure what he was up to. If there was a *bon Dieu* at all. Who could say? Then old Rosa came listing in to say *Essen ist fertig, Frau Buchner,* and we went in to lunch.

Whatever it was that I had found. Whoever it was. The painting in the book. The recurring reference in those early, embarrassing poems. The name on the lips of the beery boy at the Nass. The priest trudging down the sun-drenched Bermuda lane, and the man with the beard who met all the ships when they docked and searched all the faces. The crowing of the rooster and the sound of voices I could not quite make out in another room, and the sound of my friend's voice on the phone that I could make out all too well. My father's writing on the last page of *Gone with the Wind* that he was no good, and then, because he believed that, giving his life away for what he must have thought was our good and thus in his own sad, lost way echoing with his unimaginable gift another holy gift more unimaginable still. What I found was what I had already half seen, or less than half, in many places over my twenty-seven years without ever clearly knowing what it was that I was seeing or even that I was seeing anything of great importance. Something in me recoils from using such language, but here at the end I am left with no other way of saying it than that what I found finally was Christ. Or was found. It hardly seems to matter which. There are other words for describing what happened to me—psychological words, historical words, poetic words-but in honesty as well as in faith I am reduced to the word that is his name because no other seems to account for the experience so fully.

To say that I was born again, to use that traditional phrase, is to say too much because I remained in most ways as self-centered and squeamish after the fact as I was before, and God knows remain so still. And in another way to say that I was born again is to say too little because there have been more than a few such moments since, times when from beyond time something too precious to tell has glinted in the dusk, always just out of reach, like fireflies.

I went to see Buttrick himself the week after his sermon and told him that I found myself wondering if maybe I should go to a seminary to discover more about whatever it was that seemed to have taken place and what I should do about it, and after he asked me a few questions and pointed out that there were various roads open to me, what he did was this. He was a busy man in charge of a big and busy church, but he took his hat and coat out of the closet, handed me mine, and then drove me in his car from Madison Avenue at 73rd Street to Union Theological Seminary at Broadway and 120th Street, where I eventually entered as a student the following fall.

That made a journey of forty-seven blocks all told, not counting the long crosstown blocks at the top of the park. It was a long way to go, and there is no question but that there is a vastly longer way to go still, for all of us, before we are done. And the way we have to go is full of perils, both from without and from within, and who can say for sure what we will find at the end of our journeys, or if, when that time comes, it will prove to be anything more than such a beautiful dream as Caliban dreamed. But here at the last I find myself thinking about King Rinkitink again-another king strong in his weakness and stout of heart in the face of despair-and of those three pearls that he carried with him. The blue one that conferred such strength that no one could resist it. The pink one that protected its owner from all dangers. And the pure white one that spoke wisdom.

Faith. Hope. Love. Those are their names of course, those three-as words so worn out, but as realities so rich. Our going-away presents from beyond time to carry with us through time to lighten our step as we go. And part at least of the wisdom of the third one is, as Rinkitink heard it, "Never question the truth of what you fail to understand, for the world is filled with wonders." Above all, never question the truth beyond all understanding and surpassing all other wonders that in the long run nothing, not even the world, not even ourselves, can separate us forever from that last and deepest love that glimmers in our dusk like a pearl, like a face.

Excerpts from
Telling Secrets: A Memoir

What happened was that one of our daughters began to stop eating. There was nothing scary about it at first. It was just the sort of thing any girl who thought she'd be prettier if she lost a few pounds might do—nothing for breakfast, maybe a carrot or a Diet Coke for lunch, for supper perhaps a little salad with low calorie dressing. But then, as months went by, it did become scary. Anorexia nervosa is the name of the sickness she was suffering from, needless to say, and the best understanding of it that I have been able to arrive at goes something like this. Young people crave to be free and independent. They crave also to be taken care of and safe. The dark magic of anorexia is that it satisfies both of these cravings at once. By not eating, you take your stand against the world that is telling you what to do and who to be. And by not eating you also make your body so much smaller, lighter, weaker that in effect it becomes a child's body again and the world flocks to your rescue. This double victory is so great that apparently not even self-destruction seems too high a price to pay.

Be that as it may, she got more and more thin, of course, till she began to have the skull-like face and fleshless arms and legs of a victim of Buchenwald, and at the same time the Cowardly Lion got more and more afraid and sad, felt more and more helpless. No rational argument, no dire medical warning, no pleading or cajolery or bribery would make this young woman he loved eat normally again but only seemed to strengthen her determination not to, this young woman on whose life his own in so many ways depended. He could not solve her problem because he was of course himself part of her problem. She remained very much the same person she had always been—creative, loving, funny, bright as a star—but she was more afraid of gaining weight than she was afraid of death itself because that was what it came to finally. Three years were about as long as the sickness lasted in its most intense form with some moments when it looked as though things were getting better and some moments when it was hard to imagine they could get any worse. Then finally, when she had to be hospitalized, a doctor called one morning to say that unless they started feeding her against her will, she would die. It was as clear-cut as that. Tears ran down the Cowardly Lion's face as he stood with the telephone at his ear. His paws were tied. The bat-winged monkeys hovered.

I will not try to tell my daughter's story for two reasons. One is that it is not mine to tell but hers. The other is that of course I do not know her story, not the real story, the inside story, of what it was like for her. For the same reasons I will not try to tell what it was like for my wife or our other two children, each of whom in her own way was involved in that story. I can tell only my part in it, what happened to me, and even there I can't be sure I have it right because in many ways it is happening still. The fearsome blessing of that hard time continues to work itself out in my life in the same way we're told the universe is still hurtling through outer space under the impact of the great cosmic explosion that brought it into being in the first place. I think grace sometimes explodes into our lives like that—sending our pain, terror, astonishment hurtling through inner space until by grace they become Orion, Cassiopeia, Polaris to give us our bearings, to bring us into something like full being at last.

My anorectic daughter was in danger of starving to death, and without knowing it, so was I. I wasn't living my own life anymore because I was so caught up in hers. If in refusing to eat she was mad as a hatter, I was if anything madder still because whereas in some sense she knew what she was doing to herself, I knew nothing at all about what I was doing to myself. She had given up food. I had virtually given up doing anything in the way of feeding myself humanly. To be at peace is to have peace inside yourself more or less in spite of what is going on outside yourself. In that sense I had no peace at all. If on one particular day she took it into her head to have a slice of toast, say, with her dietetic supper, I was in seventh heaven. If on some other day she decided to have no supper at all, I was in hell.

I choose the term *hell* with some care. Hell is where there is no light but only darkness, and I was so caught up in my fear for her life, which had become in a way my life too, that none of the usual sources of light worked any more, and light was what I was starving for. I had the companionship of my wife and two other children. I read books. I played tennis and walked in the woods. I saw friends and went to the movies. But even in the midst of such times as that I remained so locked inside myself that I was not really present in them at all. Toward the end of C. S. Lewis's *The Last Battle* there is a scene where a group of dwarves sit huddled together in a tight little knot thinking that they are in a pitch black, malodorous stable when the truth of it is that they are out in the midst of an endless grassy countryside as green as Vermont with the sun shining and blue sky overhead. The huge golden lion, AsIan himself, stands nearby with all the other dwarves "kneeling in a circle around his forepaws" as Lewis writes, "and burying their hands and faces in his mane as he stooped his great head to touch them with his tongue." When AsIan offers the dwarves food, they think it is offal. When he offers them wine, they take it for ditch water. "Perfect love casteth out fear," John writes (1 John 4:18), and the other side of that is that fear like mine casteth out love, even God's love. The love I had for my daughter was lost in the anxiety I had for my daughter.

The only way I knew to be a father was to take care of her, as my father had been unable to take care of me, to move heaven and earth if necessary to make her well, and of course I couldn't do that. I didn't have either the wisdom or the power to make her well. None of us has the power to change other human beings like that, and it would be a terrible power if we did, the power to violate the humanity of others even for their own good. The psychiatrists we consulted told me I couldn't cure her. The best thing I could do for her was to stop trying to do anything. I think in my heart I knew they were right, but it didn't stop the madness of my desperate meddling, it didn't stop the madness of my trying. Everything I could think to do or say only stiffened her resolve to be free from, among other things, me. Her not eating was a symbolic way of striking out for that freedom. The only way she would ever be well again was if and when she freely chose to be. The best I could do as her father was to stand back and give her that freedom even at the risk of her using it to choose for death instead of life.

Love your neighbor as yourself is part of the great commandment. The other way to say it is, Love yourself as your neighbor. Love yourself not in some egocentric, self-serving sense but love yourself the way you would love your friend in the sense of taking care of yourself, nourishing yourself, trying to understand, comfort, strengthen yourself. Ministers in particular, people in the caring professions in general, are famous for neglecting their selves with the result that they are apt to become in their own way as helpless and crippled as the people they are trying to care for and thus no longer selves who can be of much use to anybody. If your daughter is struggling for life in a raging torrent, you do not save her by jumping into the torrent with her, which leads only to your both drowning together. Instead you keep your feet on the dry bank—you maintain as best you can your own inner peace, the best and strongest of who you are—and, from that solid ground reach out a rescuing hand. "Mind your own business" means butt out of other people's lives because in the long run they must live their lives for themselves, but it also means pay mind to your own life, your own health and wholeness, both for your own sake and ultimately for the sake of those you love too. Take care of yourself so you can take care of them. A bleeding heart is of no help to anybody if it bleeds to death.

How easy it is to write such words and how impossible it was to live them. What saved the day for my daughter was that when she finally had to be hospitalized in order to keep her alive, it happened about three thousand miles away from me. I was not there to protect her, to make her decisions, to manipulate events on her behalf, and the result was that she had to face those events on her own. There was no one to shield her from those events and their consequences in all their inexorability. In the form of doctors, nurses, social workers, the judge who determined that she was a danger to her own life and thus could be legally hospitalized against her will, society stepped in. Those men and women were not haggard, dithering, lovesick as I was. They were realistic, tough, conscientious, and in those ways, though they would never have put it in such terms themselves, loved her in a sense that I believe is closer to what Jesus meant by love than what I had been doing.

God loves in something like their way, I think. The power that created the universe and spun the dragonfly's wing and is beyond all other powers holds back, in love, from overpowering us. I have never felt God's presence more strongly than when my wife and I visited that distant hospital where our daughter was. Walking down the corridor to the room that had her name taped to the door, I felt that presence surrounding me like air—God in his very stillness, holding his breath, loving her, loving us all, the only way he can without destroying us. One night we went to compline in an Episcopal cathedral, and in the coolness and near emptiness of that great vaulted place, in the remoteness of the choir's voices chanting plainsong, in the grayness of the stone, I felt it again—the passionate restraint and hush of God.

Little by little the young woman I loved began to get well, emerging out of the shadows finally as strong and sane and wise as anybody I know, and little by little as I watched her healing happen, I began to see how much I was in need of healing and getting well myself. Like Lewis's dwarves, for a long time I had sat huddled in the dark of a stable of my own making. It was only now that I started to suspect the presence of the green countryside, the golden lion in whose image and likeness even cowardly lions are made.

This is all part of the story about what it has been like for the last ten years or so to be me, and before anybody else has the chance to ask it, I will ask it myself: Who cares? What in the world could be less important than who I am and who my father and mother were, the mistakes I have made together with the occasional discoveries, the bad times and good times, the moments of grace. If I were a public figure and my story had had some impact on the world at large, that might be some justification for telling it, but I am a very private figure indeed, living very much out of the mainstream of things in the hills of Vermont, and my life has had very little impact on anybody much except for the people closest to me and the comparative few who have read books I've written and been one, way or another touched by them.

But I talk about my life anyway because if, on the one hand, hardly anything could be less important, on the other hand, hardly anything could be more important. My story is important not because it is mine, God knows, but because if I tell it anything like right, the chances are you will recognize that in many ways it is also yours. Maybe nothing is more important than that we keep track, you and I, of these stories of who we are and where we have come from and the people we have met along the way because it is precisely through these stories in all their particularity, as I have long believed and often said, that God makes himself known to each of us most powerfully and personally. If this is true, it means that to lose track of our stories is to be profoundly impoverished not only humanly but also spiritually.

ABC's of Faith

Art

"An old silent pond.
Into the pond a frog jumps.
Splash! Silence again."

I t is perhaps the best known of all Japanese haiku. No subject could be more humdrum. No language could be more pedestrian. Basho, the poet, makes no comment on what he is describing. He implies no meaning, message, or metaphor. He simply invites our attention to no more and no less than just this: the old pond in its watery stillness, the kerplunk of the frog, the gradual return of the stillness.

In effect he is putting a frame around the moment, and what the frame does is enable us to see not just something about the moment, but the moment itself in all its ineffable ordinariness and particularity. The chances are that if we had been passing by when the frog jumped, we wouldn't have noticed a thing or, noticing it, wouldn't have given it a second thought. But the frame sets it off from everything else that distracts us. That is the nature and purpose of frames. The frame does not change the moment, but it changes our way of perceiving the moment. It makes us *notice* the moment, and that is what Basho wants above all else. It is what literature in general wants above all else too.

From the simplest lyric to the most complex novel and densest drama, literature is asking us to pay attention. Pay attention to the frog. Pay attention to the west wind. Pay attention to the boy on the raft, the lady in the tower, the old man on the train.

In sum, pay attention to the world and all that dwells therein and thereby learn at last to pay attention to yourself and all that dwells therein.

The painter does the same thing, of course. Rembrandt puts a frame around an old woman's face. It is seamed with wrinkles. The upper lip is sunken in, the skin waxy and pale. It is not a remarkable face. You would not look twice at the old woman if you found her sitting across the aisle from you on a bus. But it is a face so remarkably *seen* that it forces you to see it remarkably, just as Cezanne makes you see a bowl of apples or Andrew Wyeth a muslin curtain blowing in at an open window. It is a face unlike any other face in all the world. All the faces in the world are in this one old face.

Unlike painters, who work with space, musicians work with time, with note following note as second follows second. Listen! say Vivaldi, Brahms, Stravinsky. Listen to this time that I have framed between the first note and the last and to these sounds in time. Listen to the way the silence is broken into uneven lengths between the sounds and to the silences themselves. Listen to the scrape of bow against gut, the rap of stick against drumhead, the rush of breath through reed and wood. The sounds of the earth are like music, the old song goes, and the sounds of music are also like the sounds of the earth, which is of course where music comes from. Listen to the voices outside the window, the rumble of the furnace, the creak of your chair, the water running in the kitchen sink. Learn to listen to the music of your own lengths of time, your own silences.

Literature, painting, music—the most basic lesson that all art teaches us is to stop, look, and listen to life on this planet, including our own lives, as a vastly richer, deeper, more mysterious business than most of the time it ever occurs to us to suspect as we bumble along from day to day on automatic pilot. In a world that for the most part steers clear of the whole idea of holiness, art is one of the few places left where we can speak to each other of holy things.

Is it too much to say that to stop, look, and listen is also the most basic lesson that the Judeo-Christian tradition teaches us? Listen to history, is the cry of the ancient prophets of Israel. Listen to social injustice, says Amos; to head-in-the-sand religiosity, says Jeremiah; to international treacheries and power plays, says Isaiah; because it is precisely through them that God speaks his word of judgment and command.

And when Jesus comes along saying that the greatest command of all is to love God and to love our neighbor, he too is asking us to pay attention. If we are to love God, we must first stop, look, and listen for him in what is happening around us and inside us. I f we are to love our neighbors, before doing anything else we must see our neighbors. With our imagination as well as our eyes, that is to say like artists, we must see not just their faces, but the life behind and within their faces. Here it is love that is the frame we see them in.

In a letter to a friend Emily Dickinson wrote that "Consider the lilies of the field" was the only commandment she never broke. She could have done a lot worse. Consider the lilies. It is the sine qua non of art and religion both.

Christian

Some think a Christian is one who necessarily *believes* certain things. That Jesus was the son of God, say. Or that Mary was a virgin. Or that the pope is infallible. Or that all other religions are all wrong.

Some think a Christian is one who necessarily *does* certain things. Such as going to church. Getting baptized. Giving up liquor and tobacco. Reading the Bible. Doing a good deed a day.

Some think a Christian is just a nice person.

Jesus said, "I am the way, and the truth, and the life; no one comes to the Father, but by me" (John 14:6). He didn't say that any particular ethic, doctrine, or religion was the way, the truth, and the life. He said that he was. He didn't say that it was by believing or doing anything in particular that you could "come to the Father." He said that it was only by him—by living, participating in, being caught up by the way of life that he embodied, that was his way.

Thus it is possible to be on Christ's way and with his mark upon you without ever having heard of Christ, and for that reason to be on your way to God though maybe you don't even believe in God.

A Christian is one who is on the way, though not necessarily very far along it, and who has at least some dim and half-baked idea of whom to thank.

A Christian isn't necessarily any nicer than anybody else. Just better informed.

Eternity

Eternity is not endless time or the opposite of time. It is the essence of time.

If you spin a pinwheel fast enough, all its colors blend into a single color—white—which is the essence of all the colors of the spectrum combined.

If you spin time fast enough, time-past, time-present, and time-to-come all blend into a single timelessness or eternity, which is the essence of all times combined.

As human beings we know time as a passing of unrepeatable events in the course of which everything passes away—including ourselves. As human beings, we also know occasions when we stand outside the passing of events and glimpse their meaning. Sometimes an event occurs in our lives (a birth, a death, a marriage—some event of unusual beauty, pain, joy) through which we catch a glimpse of what our lives are all about and maybe even what life itself is all about, and this glimpse of what "it's all about" involves not just the present, but the past and future too.

Inhabitants of time that we are, we stand on such occasions with one foot in eternity. God, as Isaiah says (57:15), "inhabiteth eternity," but stands with one foot in time. The part of time where he stands most particularly is Christ, and thus in Christ we catch a glimpse of what eternity is all about, what God is all about, and what we ourselves are all about too.

Evil

- ❖ God is all-powerful.
- ❖ God is all-good.
- ❖ Terrible things happen.

You can reconcile any two of these propositions with each other, but you can't reconcile all three. The problem of evil is perhaps the greatest single problem for religious faith.

There have been numerous theological and philosophical attempts to solve it, but when it comes down to the reality of evil itself, they are none of them worth much. When a child is raped and murdered, the parents are not apt to take much comfort from the explanation (better than most) that since God wants us to love him, we must be free to love or not to love and thus free to rape and murder a child if we take a notion to.

Christian Science solves the problem of evil by saying that it does not exist except as an illusion of mortal mind. Buddhism solves it in terms of reincarnation and an inexorable law of cause and effect whereby the raped child is merely reaping the consequences of evil deeds she committed in another life.

Christianity, on the other hand, ultimately offers no theoretical solution at all. It merely points to the cross and says that, practically speaking, there is no evil so dark and so obscene—not even this—but that God can turn it to good.

Faith

When God told Abraham, who was a hundred at the time, that at the age of ninety his wife, Sarah, was finally going to have a baby, Abraham came close to knocking himself out—"fell on his face and laughed," as Genesis puts it (17:17). In another version of the story (18:8ff.), Sarah is hiding behind the door eavesdropping, and here it's Sarah herself who nearly splits a gut—although when God asks her about it afterward, she denies it. "No, but you did laugh," God says, thus having the last word as well as the first. God doesn't seem to hold their outbursts against them, however. On the contrary, God tells them the baby's going to be a boy and they are to name him Isaac. Isaac in Hebrew means "laughter."

Why did the two old crocks laugh? They laughed because they knew only a fool would believe that a woman with one foot in the grave was soon going to have her other foot in the maternity ward. They laughed because God expected them to believe it anyway. They laughed because God seemed to believe it. They laughed because they half believed it themselves. They laughed because laughing felt better than crying. They laughed because if by some crazy chance it just happened to come true, they would really have something to laugh about, and in the meanwhile it helped keep them going.

Faith is "the assurance of things hoped for, the conviction of things not seen," says the Letter to the Hebrews (11:1). Faith is laughter at the promise of a child called Laughter.

Faith is better understood as a verb than as a noun, as a process than as a possession. It is on-again-off-again rather than once-and-for-all. Faith is not being sure where you're going, but going anyway. A journey without maps. Paul Tillich said that doubt isn't the opposite of faith; it is an element of faith.

I have faith that my friend is my friend. It is possible that all his motives are ulterior. It is possible that what he is secretly drawn to is not me, but my wife or my money. But there's something about the way I feel when he's around, about the way he looks me in the eye, about the way we can talk to each other without pretense and be silent together without embarrassment, that makes me willing to put my life in his hands, as I do each time I call him friend.

I can't prove the friendship of my friend. When I experience it, I don't need to prove it. When I don't experience it, no proof will do. If I tried to put his friendship to the test somehow, the test itself would queer the friendship I was testing. So it is with the Godness of God.

The five so-called proofs for the existence of God will never prove to unfaith that God exists. They are merely five ways of describing the existence of the God you have faith in already.

Almost nothing that makes any real difference can be proved. I can prove the law of gravity by dropping a shoe out the window. I can prove that the world is round if I'm clever at that sort of thing—that the radio works, that light travels faster than sound. I cannot prove that life is better than death or love better than hate. I cannot prove the greatness of the great or the beauty of the beautiful. I cannot even prove my own free will; maybe my most heroic act, my truest love, my deepest thought are all just subtler versions of what happens when the doctor taps my knee with his little rubber hammer and my foot jumps.

Faith can't prove a damned thing. Or a blessed thing either.

Forgiveness

To forgive somebody is to say one way or another, "You have done something unspeakable, and by all rights I should call it quits between us. Both my pride and my principles demand no less. However, although I make no guarantees that I will be able to forget what you've done, and though we may both carry the scars for life, I refuse to let it stand between us. I still want you for my friend."

To accept forgiveness means to admit that you've done something unspeakable that needs to be forgiven, and thus both parties must swallow the same thing: their pride.

This seems to explain what Jesus means when he says to God, "Forgive us our trespasses as we forgive those who trespass against us." Jesus is not saying that God's forgiveness is conditional upon our forgiving others. In the first place, forgiveness that's conditional isn't really forgiveness at all, just fair warning; and in the second place, our unforgivingness is among those things about us that we need to have God forgive us most. What Jesus apparently is saying is that the pride that keeps us from forgiving is the same pride that keeps us from accepting forgiveness, and will God please help us do something about it.

When somebody you've wronged forgives you, you're spared the dull and self-diminishing throb of a guilty conscience.

When you forgive somebody who has wronged you, you're spared the dismal corrosion of bitterness and wounded pride.

For both parties, forgiveness means the freedom again to be at peace inside their own skins and to be glad in each other's presence.

God

There must be a God because (a) since the beginning of history, the most variegated majority of people have intermittently believed there was; (b) it is hard to consider the vast and complex structure of the universe in general and of the human mind in particular without considering the possibility that they issued from some ultimate source, itself vast, complex, and somehow mindful; (c) built into the very being of even the most primitive human there seems to be a profound psychophysical need or hunger for something like truth, goodness, love, and—under one alias or another—for God; and (d) every age and culture has produced mystics who have experienced a Reality beyond reality and have come back using different words and images but obviously and without collusion describing with awed adoration the same Indescribability.

Statements of this sort and others like them have been advanced for several thousand years as proofs of the existence of God. A twelve-year-old child can see that no one of them is watertight. And even all of them taken together won't convince any of us unless our predisposition to be convinced outweighs our predisposition not to be.

It is as impossible to prove or disprove that God exists beyond the various and conflicting ideas people have dreamed up about God as it is to prove or disprove that goodness exists beyond the various and conflicting ideas people have dreamed up about what is good.

It is as impossible for us to demonstrate the existence of God as it would be for even Sherlock Holmes to demonstrate the existence of Arthur Conan Doyle.

All-wise. All-powerful. All-loving. All-knowing. We bore to death both God and ourselves with our chatter. God cannot be expressed, only experienced.

Grace

After centuries of handling and mishandling, most religious words have become so shopworn nobody's much interested anymore. Not so with *grace*, for some reason. Mysteriously, even derivatives like *gracious* and *graceful* still have some of the bloom left.

Grace is something you can never get but can only be given. There's no way to earn it or deserve it or bring it about any more than you can deserve the taste of raspberries and cream or earn good looks or bring about your own birth.

A good sleep is grace and so are good dreams. Most tears are grace. The smell of rain is grace. Somebody loving you is grace. Loving somebody is grace. Have you ever *tried* to love somebody?

A crucial eccentricity of the Christian faith is the assertion that people are saved by grace. There's nothing *you* have to do. There's nothing you *have* to do. There's nothing you have to *do*.

The grace of God means something like: "Here is your life. You might never have been, but you *are*, because the party wouldn't have been complete without you. Here is the world. Beautiful and terrible things will happen. Don't be afraid. I am with you. Nothing can ever separate us. It's for you I created the universe. I love you."

There's only one catch. Like any other gift, the gift of grace can be yours only if you'll reach out and take it.

Maybe being able to reach out and take it is a gift too.

Homosexuality

One of the many ways that we are attracted to each other is sexually. We want to touch and be touched. We want to give and receive pleasure with our bodies. We want to know each other in our full nakedness, which is to say in our full humanness, and in the moment of passion to become one with each other. Whether it is our own gender or the other that we are chiefly attracted to seems a secondary matter. There is a female element in every male just as there is a male element in every female, and most people, if they're honest, will acknowledge having been at one time or another attracted to both.

To say that morally, spiritually, humanly, homosexuality is always bad seems as absurd as to say that in the same terms heterosexuality is always good, or the other way round. It is not the object of our sexuality that determines its value but the inner nature of our sexuality. If (a) it is as raw as the coupling of animals, at its worst it demeans us and at its best still leaves our deepest hunger for each other unsatisfied. If (b) it involves some measure of kindness, understanding, and affection as well as desire, it can become an expression of human love in its fullness and can thus help to complete us as humans. Whatever our sexual preference happens to be, both of these possibilities are always there. It's not whom you go to bed with or what you do when you get there that matters so much. It's what besides sex you are asking to receive, and what besides sex you are offering to give.

Here and there the Bible condemns homosexuality in the sense of (a), just as under the headings of adultery and fornication it also condemns heterosexuality in the sense of (a). On the subject of homosexuality in the sense of (b), it is as silent as it is on the subject of sexuality generally in the sense of (b). The great commandment is that we are to love one another—responsibly, faithfully, joyfully—and presumably the biblical view is implied in that.

Beyond that, "Love is strong as death," sings Solomon in his song. "Many waters cannot quench love, neither can floods drown it" (Song of Solomon 8:6-7). Whoever you are and whoever it is you desire, the passion of those lines is something you are quick to recognize.

The Lord's Prayer

In the Episcopal order of worship, the priest sometimes introduces the Lord's Prayer with the words, "Now, as our Savior Christ hath taught us, we are bold to say..." The word *bold* is worth thinking about. We do well not to pray the prayer lightly. It takes guts to pray it at all. We can pray it in the unthinking and perfunctory way we usually do only by disregarding what we are saying.

"Thy will be done" is what we are saying. That is the climax of the first half of the prayer. We are asking God to be God. We are asking God to do not what we want, but what God wants. We are asking God to make manifest the holiness that is now mostly hidden, to set free in all its terrible splendor the devastating power that is now mostly under restraint. "Thy kingdom come . . . on earth" is what we are saying. And if that were suddenly to happen, what then? What would stand and what would fall? Who would be welcomed in and who would be thrown the hell out? Which if any of our most precious visions of what God is and of what human beings are would prove to be more or less on the mark and which would turn out to be phony as three-dollar bills? Boldness indeed. To speak those words is to invite the tiger out of the cage, to unleash a power that makes atomic power look like a warm breeze.

You need to be bold in another way to speak the second half. Give us. Forgive us. Don't test us. Deliver us. If it takes guts to face the omnipotence that is God's, it takes perhaps no less to face the impotence that is ours. We can do nothing without

God. We can have nothing without God. Without God we are nothing.

It is only the words "Our Father" that make the prayer bearable. If God is indeed something like a father, then as something like children maybe we can risk approaching him anyway.

Observance

A religious observance can be a wedding, a christening, a Memorial Day service, a bar mitzvah, or anything like that you might be apt to think of. There are lots of things going on at them. There are lots of things you can learn from them if you're in a receptive state of mind. The word *observance* itself suggests what is perhaps the most important thing about them.

A man and a woman are getting married. A child is being given a name. A war is being remembered and many deaths. A youngster is coming of age.

It is life that is going on. It is always going on, and it is always precious. It is God that is going on. It is you who are there that is going on.

As Henry James advised writers, be one on whom nothing is lost.

Observe!! There are few things as important, as religious, as that.

Remember

When you remember me, it means that you have carried something of who I am with you, that I have left some mark of who I am on who you are. It means that you can summon me back to your mind even though countless years and miles may stand between us. It means that if we meet again, you will know me. It means that even after I die, you can still see my face and hear my voice and speak to me in your heart.

For as long as you remember me, I am never entirely lost. When I'm feeling most ghostlike, it's your remembering me that helps remind me that I actually exist. When I'm feeling sad, it's my consolation. When I'm feeling happy, it's part of why I feel that way.

If you forget me, one of the ways I remember who I am will be gone. If you forget me, part of who I am will be gone.

"Jesus, remember me when you come into your kingdom," the good thief said from his cross (Luke 23:42). There are perhaps no more human words in all of Scripture, no prayer we can pray so well.

Tears

You never know what may cause tears. The sight of the Atlantic Ocean can do it, or a piece of music, or a face you've never seen before. A pair of somebody's old shoes can do it. Almost any movie made before the great sadness that came over the world after the Second World War, a horse cantering across a meadow, the high-school basketball team running out onto the gym floor at the start of a game. You can never be sure. But of this you can be sure. Whenever you find tears in your eyes, especially unexpected tears, it is well to pay the closest attention.

They are not only telling you something about the secret of who you are, but more often than not God is speaking to you through them of the mystery of where you have come from and is summoning you to where, if your soul is to be saved, you should go to next.

Trinity

The much maligned doctrine of the Trinity is an assertion that, appearances to the contrary notwithstanding, there is only one God.

Father, Son, and Holy Spirit mean that the mystery beyond us, the mystery among us, and the mystery within us are all the same mystery. Thus the Trinity is a way of saying something about us and the way we experience God.

The Trinity is also a way of saying something about God and God's inner nature; that is, God does not need the creation in order to have something to love, because within God's being love happens. In other words, the love God is is love not as a noun, but as a verb. This verb is reflexive as well as transitive.

If the idea of God as both Three and One seems farfetched and obfuscating, look in the mirror someday.

There is (a) the interior life known only to yourself and those you choose to communicate it to (the Father). There is (b) the visible face, which in some measure reflects that inner life (the Son). And there is (c) the invisible power you have that enables you to communicate that interior life in such a way that others do not merely know about it, but know it in the sense of its becoming part of who they are (the Holy Spirit). Yet what you are looking at in the mirror is clearly and indivisibly the one and only you.

Vocation

Vocation comes from the Latin *vocare*. "to call," means the work a person is called to by God.

There are all different kinds of voices calling you to all different kinds of work, and the problem is to find out which is the voice of God rather than of society, say, or the superego, or self-interest.

By and large a good rule for finding out is this: The kind of work God usually calls you to is the kind of work (a) that you need to do and (b) that the world needs to have done. If you really get a kick out of your work, you've presumably met requirement (a), but if your work is writing cigarette ads, the chances are you've missed requirement (b). On the other hand, if your work is being a doctor in a leper colony, you have probably met requirement (b), but if most of the time you're bored and depressed by it, the chances are you have not only bypassed (a), but probably aren't helping your patients much either.

Neither the hair shirt nor the soft berth will do. The place God calls you to is the place where your deep gladness and the world's deep hunger meet.

Lectures & Sermons

Faith and Fiction

A year or so ago, a friend of mine died. He was an Englishman—witty, elegant, multifaceted. One morning in his sixty-eighth year he simply didn't wake up. It was about as easy a way as he could possibly have done it, but it was not easy for the people he left behind because it gave us no chance to start getting used to the idea beforehand or to say good-bye either in words, if we turned out to be up to it, or in some awkward, unspoken way if we weren't. He died in March, and in May my wife and I were staying with his widow overnight when I had a short dream about him. I dreamed he was standing there in the dark guest room where we were asleep, looking very much himself in the navy blue jersey and white slacks he often wore. I told him how much we had missed him and how glad I was to see him again. He acknowledged that somehow. Then I said, "Are you really there, Dudley?" I meant was he there in fact, in truth, or was I merely dreaming he was. His answer was that he was really there. "Can you prove it?" I asked him. "Of course," he said. Then he plucked a strand of wool out of his jersey and tossed it to me. I caught it between my thumb and forefinger, and the feel of it was so palpably real that it woke me up. That's all there was to it. It was as if he'd come on purpose to do what he'd done and then left. I told the dream at breakfast the next morning, and I'd hardly finished when my wife spoke. She said that she'd seen the strand on the carpet as she was getting dressed. She was sure it hadn't been there the night before. I rushed upstairs to see for myself, and there it was—a little tangle of navy blue wool.

Another event. I went into a bar in an airport not long ago to fortify myself against my least favorite means of transportation. It was an off hour, so I was the only customer and had a choice of the whole row of empty bar stools. On the counter in front of each of them was a holder with a card stuck in it advertising the drink of the day or something like that. I noticed that the one in front of me had a small metal piece on top of the card that wasn't on the others, so I took a look at it. It turned out to be a tie clip that somebody must have stuck there. It had three letters engraved on it, and the letters were C.F.B. Those are my initials.

Lastly this. I was receiving Communion in an Episcopal church early one morning. The priest was an acquaintance of mine. I could hear him moving along the rail from person to person as I knelt there waiting my turn. The body of Christ, he said, the bread of heaven. The body of Christ, the bread of heaven. When he got to me, he put in another word. The word was my name. "The body of Christ, Freddy, the bread of heaven."

The dream about my friend may well have been just another dream, and you certainly don't have to invoke the supernatural to account for the thread on the carpet. The tie clip I find harder to explain away. It seems to me that, mathematically speaking, the odds against its having not just one or two but all three of my initials on it in the right order must be astronomical, but I suppose that could be just a coincidence too. On the other hand, in both cases there is the other possibility too. Far-out or not, I don't see how any open-minded person can a priori deny it, and in a way it is that other possibility, as a possibility, that is at the heart of everything I want to say here.

Maybe my friend really did come to me in my dream and the thread was his sign to me that he had. Maybe it is true that by God's grace the dead are given back their lives again and that the doctrine of the resurrection of the body is not just a doctrine. He couldn't have looked more substantial and less ectoplasmic standing there in the dark, and it was such a crisp, no-nonsense exchange we had, with nothing surreal or wispy about it. It was so much like him. As to the tie clip, it seemed so extraordinary that for a moment I almost refused to believe it had happened at all. I think that's worth marking. Even though I had the thing right there in my hand, my first inclination was to deny it for the simple reason, I suspect, that it was so unsettling to my whole commonsense view of the way the world works that it was easier and less confusing just to shrug it off as a crazy fluke. I think we are all inclined to do that. But maybe it wasn't a fluke. Maybe it was a crazy little peek behind the curtain, a dim little whisper of providence from the wings. I had been expected. I was on schedule. I was taking the right journey at the right time. I was not alone.

What happened at the Communion rail was rather different. There was nothing extraordinary about the priest's knowing my name—I knew he knew it—and there was nothing extraordinary about his using it in the service either, I learned later, because it was a practice he not infrequently followed.

But its effect upon me was extraordinary. It caught me off guard. It moved me deeply. For the first time in my life perhaps it struck me that when Jesus picked up the bread at his last meal and said, "This is my body, which is for you," he was doing it not just in a ritual way for humankind in general but in an unthinkably personal way for every particular man, woman, child who ever existed or someday would exist. Most unthinkable of all, as far as I was concerned, maybe he was doing it for me. At that holiest of feasts, we are known not just by our official names but by the names people use who have known us longest and most intimately. We are welcomed not as the solid citizens that our Sunday best suggests we are, but in all our inner tackiness and tatteredness that no one in the world knows better than we each of us know it about ourselves-the bitterness, the phoniness, the confusion, the irritability, the prurience, the half-heartedness. The bread of heaven, *Freddy*, of all people? Molly? Bill? Ridiculous little What's-her-name? Boring old So-and-so? Extraordinary. It seemed a revelation from on high. Was it?

All that's extraordinary about these three minor events is the fuss I've made about them. Things like that happen every day to everybody. They are a dime a dozen. They mean absolutely nothing. Or things like that are momentary glimpses into a Mystery of such depth, power, and beauty that if we were to see it head-on, we would be annihilated.

If I had to bet my life on one possibility or the other, which one would I bet it on? If you had to bet your life, which one would you bet it on? On Yes, there is God in the highest, or, if such language is no longer viable, there is Mystery and Meaning in the deepest? On No, there is whatever happens to happen, and it means whatever you choose it to mean, and that is all there is?

We may bet Yes this evening and No tomorrow morning. We may know we are betting or we may not know. We may bet one way with our lips, our minds, our hearts even, and another way with our feet. But we all of us bet, and it's our lives themselves we're betting with in the sense that the betting is what shapes our lives. And we can never be sure we've bet right, of course. The evidence both ways is fragmentary, fragile, ambiguous. A coincidence can be, as somebody has said, God's way of remaining anonymous, or it can be just a coincidence. Is the dream that brings healing and hope just a product of wishful thinking? Or is it a message from another world? Whether we bet Yes or No, it is equally an act of faith.

Religious faith, the Letter to the Hebrews says in a famous chapter, "is the assurance of things hoped for, the conviction of things not seen" (11: 1). Noah, Abraham, Sarah, and the rest of them it goes on to say, "all died in faith, not having received what was promised, bur having seen it and greeted it from afar, and having acknowledged that they were strangers and exiles on the earth. For people [like that] make it clear that they are seeking a homeland" (11:13-14).

Faith, therefore, is distinctly different from other aspects of the religious life and not to be confused with them even though we sometimes use the word to mean religious belief in general, as in phrases like "the Christian faith" or "the faith of Islam." Faith is different from theology because theology is reasoned, systematic, and orderly, whereas faith is disorderly, intermittent, and full of surprises. Faith is different from mysticism because mystics in their ecstasy become one with what faith can at most see only from afar. Faith is different from ethics because ethics is primarily concerned not, like faith, with our relationship to God but with our relationship to each other. Faith is closest perhaps to worship because like worship it is essentially a response to God and involves the emotions and the physical senses as well as the mind, but worship is consistent, structured, single-minded and seems to know what it's doing while faith is a stranger and exile on the earth and doesn't know for certain about anything. Faith is homesickness. Faith is a lump in the throat. Faith is less a position *on* than a movement *toward*, less a sure thing than a hunch. Faith is waiting. Faith is journeying through space and through time.

If someone were to come up and ask me to talk about my faith, it is exactly that journey that I would eventually have to talk about—the ups and downs of the years, the dreams, the odd moments, the intuitions. I would have to talk about the occasional sense I have that life is not just a series of events causing other events as haphazardly as a break shot in pool causes the billiard balls to career off in all directions but that life has a plot the way a novel has a plot, that events are somehow or other leading somewhere. Whatever your faith may be or my faith may be, it seems to me inseparable from the story of what has happened to us, and that is why I believe that no literary form is better adapted to the subject than the form of fiction.

Faith and fiction both journey forward in time and space and draw their life from the journey, *are* in fact the journey. Faith and fiction both involve the concrete, the earthen, the particular more than they do the abstract and cerebral. In both, the people you meet along the way, the things that happen, the places—the airport bar, the room where you have your last supper with a friend—count for more than ideas do. Fiction can hold opposites together simultaneously like love and hate, laughter and tears, despair and hope, and so of course does faith, which by its very nature both sees and does not see and whose most characteristic utterance, perhaps, is "Lord, I believe; help thou my unbelief" (Mark 9:24, KJV). Faith and fiction both start once upon a time and are continually changing and growing in mood, intensity, and direction. When faith stops changing and growing, it dies on its feet. So does fiction. And they have more in common than that.

They both start with a leap in the dark, for one. How can Noah, Abraham, Sarah, or anyone else know for sure that the promise they die without receiving will ever be kept and that their journey in search of a homeland will ever get them there? How can anybody writing a novel or a story know for sure where it will lead and just how and with what effect it will end or even if it is a story worth telling? Let writers beware who from the start know too much about what they are doing and keep too heavy a hand on the reins. They leave too little room for luck as they tell their stories, just the way Abraham and Sarah, if they know too much about what they are doing as they *live* their stories, leave too little room for grace.

The word *fiction* comes from a Latin verb meaning "to shape, fashion, feign." That is what fiction does, and in many ways it is what faith does too. You fashion your story, as you fashion your faith, out of the great hodgepodge of your life—the things that have happened to you and the things you have dreamed of happening. They are the raw material of both. Then, if you're a writer like me, you try less to impose a shape on the hodgepodge than to see what shape emerges from it, is hidden in it. You try to sense what direction it is moving in. You listen to it. You avoid forcing your characters to march too steadily to the drumbeat of your artistic purpose, but leave them some measure of real freedom to be themselves. If minor characters show signs of becoming major characters, you at least give them a shot at it because in the world of fiction it may take many pages before you find out who the major characters really are just as in the real world it may take you many years to find out that the stranger you talked to for half an hour once in a railway station may have done more to point you to where your true homeland lies than your closest friend or your psychiatrist.

As a writer I use such craft as I have at my command, of course. I figure out what scenes to put in and, just as important, what scenes to leave out. I decide when to use dialogue and spend hours trying to make it sound like human beings talking to each other instead of just me talking to myself. I labor to find the right tone of voice to tell my story in, which is to say the right style, ultimately the right word, which is the most demanding part of it all—sentence after sentence, page after page, looking for the word that has freshness and power and life in it. But I try not to let my own voice be the dominant one. The limitation of the great stylists, of course—of a James, say, or a Hemingway—is that it is their voices you remember long after you have forgotten the voices of any of their characters. "Be still, and know that I am God," is the advice of the psalmist (46:10), and I've always taken it to be good literary advice too. Be still the way Tolstoy is still, or Anthony Trollope is still, so your characters can speak for themselves and come alive in their own way.

In faith and fiction both you *fashion* out of the raw stuff of your experience. If you want to remain open to the luck and grace of things anyway, you *shape* that stuff in the sense less of imposing a shape on it than of discovering the shape. And in both you *feign*—feigning as imagining, as making visible images for invisible things. Fiction can't be true the way a photograph is true, but at its best it can feign truth the way a good portrait does, inward and invisible truth. Fiction at its best can be true to the experience of being a human in this world, and the fiction you write depends, needless to say, on the part of that experience you choose. The part that has always most interested me is best illustrated by such incidents as the three I described at the outset. The moment that unaccountably brings tears to your eyes, that takes you by crazy surprise, that sends a shiver down your spine, that haunts you with what is just possibly a glimpse of something far beyond or deep within itself That is the part of the human experience I choose to write about in my fiction. It is the part I am most concerned to feign, that is, make images for. In that sense I can live with the label of religious novelist. In any other sense, it is a label that makes my flesh crawl.

I lean over backwards not to preach or propagandize in my fiction. I don't dream up plots and characters to illustrate some homiletic message. I am not bent on driving home some theological point. I am simply trying to conjure up stories in which people are touched with what may or may not be the presence of God in their lives as I believe we all of us are even though we might sooner be shot dead than use that kind of language to describe it. In my own experience, the ways God appears in our lives are elusive and ambiguous always. There is always room for doubt in order, perhaps, that there will always be room to breathe. There is so much in life that hides God and denies the very possibility of God that there are times when it is hard not to deny God altogether. Yet it is possible to have faith nonetheless. Faith is that Nonetheless. That is the experience I am trying to be true to in the same way that other novelists try to be true to the experience of being a woman, say, or an infantryman in World War II. In all of them, there is perhaps nothing more crucial than honesty.

If you are going to be a religious novelist, you have got to be honest not just about the times that glimmer with God's presence but also about the ones that are dark with his absence, because needless to say you have had your dark times like everybody else. Terrible things happen in the four novels *(Lion Country, Open Heart, Love Feast,* and *Treasure Hunt)* I wrote about Leo Bebb. In a drunken fit, Bebb's wife, Lucille, kills her own baby, and when Bebb tells her long afterwards that she has been washed dean in the blood of the Lamb, she answers him by saying, "Bebb, the only thing I've been washed in is the shit of the horse," and dies a suicide. Poor Brownie, reeking of aftershave, decides in the end that his rose-colored faith in the goodness of things is as false as his china choppers and loses it. Miriam Parr dies of cancer wondering if she is "going someplace," as she puts it, or "just out like a match." The narrator is a rather feckless, rootless young man named Antonio Parr, who starts out in the first book with no sense of commitment to anything or anybody but who, through his relationship with Leo Bebb, gradually comes alive to at least the possibility of something like religious faith. He has learned to listen for God in the things that happen to him anyway, just in case there happens to be a God to listen for. Maybe all he can hear, he says, is "Time's winged chariot hurrying near." Or, if there is more to it than that, the most he can say of it constitutes the passage with which the last of the four novels ends, in which he uses the Lone Ranger as an image for Christ: "To be honest, I must say that on occasion I hear something else too—not the thundering of distant hoofs, maybe, or *Hi-yo, Silver. Away!* echoing across the lonely sage, but the faint chunk-chunk of my own moccasin heart, of the Tonto afoot in the dusk of me somewhere who, not because he ought to but because he can't help himself, whispers *Kemo Sabe* every once in a while to what may or may not be only a silvery trick of the failing light."

Terrible things as well as wonderful things happen in those books, but it's not so much that I have to cook them up in order to give a balanced view of the way life is as it is that they have a way of happening as much on their own in the fictional world as in the real world. If you're preaching or otherwise grinding an axe, you let happen, of course, only the things you want to have happen; but insofar as fiction, like faith, is a journey not only forward in space and time, but a journey inward, it is full of surprises. Even the wonderful things—the things that religious writers in the propagandist sense would presumably orchestrate and control most of all—tend at their best to come as a surprise, and that is what is most wonderful about them. In the case of the Bebb books again, for instance, I was well along into *Lion Country,* the first of them, before I came to the surprising conclusion that Bebb himself was, wonderfully, a saint.

Imagine setting out consciously to write a novel about a saint. How could you avoid falling flat on your face? Nothing is harder to make real than holiness. Certainly nothing is harder to make appealing and attractive. The danger, I suppose, is that you start out with the idea that sainthood is something people achieve, that you get to be holy more or less the way you get to be an Eagle Scout. To create a saint from that point of view would be to end up with something on the order of Little Nell.

The truth, of course, is that holiness is not a human quality like virtue. If there is such a thing at all, holiness is Godness and as such is not something people do but something God does in them, if there is such a thing as God. It is something God seems especially apt to do in people who are not virtuous at all, at least not to start with. Think of Francis of Assisi or Mary Magdalene. Quite the contrary. If you're too virtuous, the chances are you think you are a saint already under your own steam, and therefore the real thing can never happen to you. Leo Bebb was not an Eagle Scout. He ran a religious diploma mill and ordained people through the mail for a fee. He did five years in the pen on a charge of indecent exposure involving children. He had a child by the wife of his twin brother. But he was a risk-taker. He was as round and fat and as full of bounce as a rubber ball. He was without pretense. He was good company. Above all else, he was extraordinarily alive—so much so for me anyway that when I was writing about him I could hardly wait to get back to my study every morning. That's when I began not only to see that he was a saint, but to see also what a saint is.

A saint is a life-giver. I hadn't known that before. A saint is a human being with the same sorts of hang-ups and abysses as the rest of us, but if a saint touches your life, you become alive in a new way. Even aimless, involuted Antonio Parr came more alive through knowing Bebb though at first he was out to expose him as a charlatan. So did the theosophist Gertrude Conover, Bebb's blue-haired octogenarian paramour. More extraordinary yet, I came more alive myself I am a bookish, private sort of man, but in my old age I find myself doing and saying all sorts of outrageous things that, before Bebb came into my life and my fiction, I would have never even considered. I didn't think Bebb up at all the way he finally emerged as a character—sometimes I wonder if he was the one who thought me up. I had another kind of character in mind entirely when I started. In his tightfitting raincoat and Tyrolean hat, he simply turned out to be the person he was in the journey of writing those books. I didn't expect him. I didn't deserve him. He came making no conditions. There were no strings attached. He was a free gift.

That is also what grace is—to use the religious word for it. Grace is God in his givenness. Faith is not *sui generis*. It is a response to the givenness of grace. Faith is given a glimpse of *something*, however dimly. Men and women of faith know they are strangers and exiles on the earth because somehow and somewhere along the line they have been given a glimpse of home. Maybe the little tangle of navy blue wool on the carpet was grace, even if it could be proved that it had only come from my own sweater. By grace we see what we see. To have faith is to respond to what we see by longing for it the rest of our days; by trying to live up to it and toward it through all the wonderful and terrible things; by breathing it in like air and growing strong on it; by looking to see it again and see it better. To lose faith is to stop looking. To lose faith is to decide, like Brownie, that all you ever saw from afar was your own best dreams.

The whole idea of the Muse is another way of speaking of this same matter of course, the goddess who inspires. And the word "inspiration" itself as a *breathing into* is another. In fiction as in faith something from outside ourselves is breathed into us if we're lucky, if we're open enough to inhale it. I think writers of religious fiction especially have to stay open in that way. They've got to play their hunches more and take risks more. They shouldn't try to keep too tight a rein on what they're doing. They should be willing to be less professional and literary and more eccentric, antic, disheveled—less like John Updike or Walker Percy, maybe, and more like Kurt Vonnegut, or Peter de Vries, or G. K. Chesterton. In the stories of Flannery O'Connor, for instance, I have a sense of the author herself being caught off guard by a flash of insight here, a stab of feeling there. She is making discoveries about holy things and human things in a way that I think would never have been possible if she had known too well where she was going and how she was going to get there; and as her readers we share in the freshness and wonder of her surprise. I suppose *The Brothers Karamazov* would be the classic example of what I'm talking about—that great seething bouillabaisse of a book. It is digressive and sprawling, with many too many characters in it and much too long, and yet it is a book that, just because Dostoevsky leaves room in it for whatever comes up to enter, is entered here and there by maybe no less than the Holy Spirit itself, thereby becoming, as far as I am concerned, what at its best a religious novel can be—that is to say a novel less *about* the religious experience than a novel the reading of which itself *is* a religious experience—of God both in his subterranean presence and in his appalling absence.

Is it the Holy Spirit? Is it the Muse? Is it just a lucky break? Who dares say without crossing the fingers. But as in the journey of faith it is possible every once and a while to be better than you are—"Do you not know that … God's Spirit dwells within you?" Paul asks (1 Cor. 3:16)—in the journey of fiction-making it is possible to write more than you know. Bebb was a saint—a kind of saint anyway—and when I finally finished with him, or he with me, I found that it was very hard to write a novel about any other kind of person. I tried a fifteenth-century alchemist, a twentieth-century woman novelist, a dishwasher in a New England restaurant, an old lady in a nursing home, and one by one they failed to come to life for me. They were all in their own ways too much like me, I suppose, and after so many years I have come to be a little tired of me. And too many other authors were writing novels about people like that, many of them better than I could do it, so why add to the number? Then I realized that, more even than those reasons, the basic reason none of them worked for me was that, after Bebb, only saints really interest me as a writer.

There is so much life in them. They are so in touch with, so transparent to, the mystery of things that you never know what to expect from them. Anything is possible for a saint. They won't stay put or be led around by the nose no matter how hard you try. And then entirely by accident one day—or by grace, or by luck—I came across a historical saint whom I'd never heard of before even by name. He was born in England in 1065 and died there in 1170. His name was Godric.

If like me, you don't happen to be a saint yourself I don't know how you write about one without being given something from somewhere. That is especially true if you try, as I did, to make the saint himself your narrator so that you have his whole interior life on your hands as well as his career. Add to that, Godric was a man who was born close to a thousand years ago—lived in a different world, spoke a different language, saw things in a different way. I did some research, needless to say—not of the thoroughgoing sort that I assume a real historical novelist undertakes, because it wasn't primarily the historical period that I was interested in but, rather, Godric himself. Nonetheless I read enough to give myself some idea of roughly what was going on in Europe at the time, especially in England. Largely through the ineffable *Dictionary of National Biography,* I found out what I could about such historical figures who played parts in Godric's life as Abbot Ailred of Rievaulx Abbey and Ranulf Flambard, bishop of Durham and former chancellor to William II. I tried with meager success to find out what Rome and Jerusalem looked like when Godric made his pilgrimages there. I dug a little into the First Crusade because Godric was briefly involved with it apparently. The principal source on Godric himself is a contemporary biography written by a monk known as Reginald of Durham, who knew him and who figures as a character in the novel.

The book has never been translated from medieval Latin, and in that regard something rather remarkable happened comparable to the discovery of the tie clip with my initials on it. My own Latin came to an end with Caesar's *Commentaries* some fifty years ago, so the best I could do was to look up promising references in the English index and then try to get at least the gist of them with the help of a dictionary. Then, just as I was getting started on that, one of my daughters, who was off at boarding school, phoned to ask if she could bring some friends home for the weekend, and one of the friends turned out to be chairman of the school's classics department. I suppose he was the only person within a radius of a hundred miles or more who could have done the job, and both evenings he was with us he gave me sight translations of the passages I was after.

But I am talking about something even odder than that and more precious. I am talking about how, by something like grace, you are given every once in a while to be better than you are and to write more than you know. Less because of the research I did than in spite of it, Godric came alive for me—that is what I was given: the way he thought, the way he spoke, the humanness of him, the holiness of him. I don't believe any writer can do that just by taking thought and effort and using the customary tools of the craft. Something else has to happen more mysterious than that. Godric not only came alive for me, but he came speaking words that had a life and a twist to them that I can't feel entirely responsible for. I don't want to make it sound spookier than it was. I was the one who wrote his words, of course. In some sense I invented them, dredged them up out of some subbasement of who I am. But the words were more like him than they were like me, and without him I feel certain I could never have found them and written them.

Year after year as a hermit in the north of England, the old man used to chasten his flesh in all seasons by bathing in the river Wear a few miles out of Durham. When he got too feeble to do that, he had a servant dig a hole in the chapel he had built for the Virgin Mary and fill it with water from the river so he could still bathe in it there. Here is a passage from the novel in which he describes what it was like both to bathe in the river in midwinter and, later, to bathe in the little pool of it in the chapel:

> First there's the fiery sting of cold that almost stops my breath, the aching torment in my limbs. I think I may go mad, my wits so outraged that they seek to flee my skull like rats a ship that's going down. I puff. I gasp. Then inch by inch a blessed numbness comes. I have no legs, no arms. My very heart grows still. These floating hands are not my hands. This ancient flesh I wear is rags for all I feel of it.

> "Praise, praise!" I croak: Praise God for all that's holy, cold, and dark. Praise him for all we lose, for all the river of the years bears off. Praise him for stillness in the wake of pain. Praise him for emptiness. And as you race to spill into the sea, praise him yourself, old Wear. Praise him for dying and the peace of death.

> In the little church I built of wood for Mary, I hollowed out a place for him. Perkin brings him by

the pail and pours him in. Now that I can hardly walk, I crawl to meet him there. He takes me in his chilly lap to wash me of my sins. Or I kneel down beside him till within his depths I see a star.

Sometimes this star is still. Sometimes she dances. She is Mary's star. Within that little pool of Wear she winks at me. I wink at her. The secret that we share I cannot tell in full. But this much I will tell. What's lost is nothing to what's found, and all the death that ever was, set next to life, would scarcely fill a cup.

Feigning is part of it. Imagining, image-making. Reaching deep. But it feels like more than that. Godric told me things I didn't know. He revealed something of himself to me and something of the distant past. He also revealed something of myself to me and something of the not so distant future. I will grow old. I will die. I think it was through his eyes that I first saw beyond the inevitability of it to the mercy of it. "All's lost. All's found." I have faith that that is true, or someday will turn out to be true, but on the old saint's lips the words have a ring of certitude and benediction from which I draw courage as I think I could not from any words merely of my own.

Is that why we write, people like me—to keep our courage up? Are novels such as mine a kind of whistling in the dark? I think so. To whistle in the dark is more than just to try to *convince* yourself that dark is not all there is. It is also to *remind* yourself that dark is not all there is or the end of all there is because even in the dark there is hope. Even in the dark you have the power to whistle, and sometimes that seems more than just your own power, because it is powerful enough to hold the dark back. The tunes you whistle in the dark are the images you make of that hope, that power. They are the books you write.

In just the same way faith could be called a kind of whistling in the dark too, of course. The living out of faith. The writing out of fiction. In both you shape, you fashion, you feign. Maybe what they have most richly in common is a way of paying attention. Page by page, chapter by chapter, the story unfolds. Day by day, year by year, your own story unfolds, your life's story. Things happen. People come and go. The scene shifts. Time runs by, runs out. Maybe it is all utterly meaningless. Maybe it is all unutterably meaningful. If you want to know which, pay attention. What it means to be truly human in a world that half the time we are in love with and half the time scares the hell out of us—any fiction that helps us pay attention to that is as far as I am concerned religious fiction.

The unexpected sound of your name on somebody's lips. The good dream. The odd coincidence. The moment that brings tears to your eyes. The person who brings life to your life. Maybe even the smallest events hold the greatest dues. If it is God we are looking for, as I suspect we all of us are even if we don't think of it that way and wouldn't use such language on a bet, maybe the reason we haven't found him is that we are not looking in the right places.

Pay attention. *As* a summation of all that I have had to say as a writer, I would settle for that. And as a talisman or motto for that journey in search of a homeland, which is what faith is, I would settle for that too.

A Room Called Remember

And they brought in the ark of God, and set it inside the tent which David had pitched for it; and they offered burnt offerings and peace offerings before God.... Then on that day David first appointed that thanksgiving be sung to the Lord by Asaph and his brethren: "0 give thanks to the Lord, call on his name, make known his deeds among the peoples! ... Glory in his holy name; let the hearts of those who seek the Lord rejoice! Seek the Lord and his strength, seek his presence continually! Remember the wonderful works that he has done, the wonders he wrought, the judgments he uttered."

-1 CHRONICLES 16:1, 7-12

And he said, "Jesus, remember me when you come in your kingly power." And he said to him, "Truly, I say to you, today you will be with me in Paradise."

-LUKE 23:42-43

very once in a while, if you're like me, you have a dream that wakes you up. Sometimes it's a bad dream—a dream in which the shadows become so menacing that your heart skips a beat and you come awake to the knowledge that not even the actual darkness of night is as fearsome as the dreamed darkness, not even the shadows without as formidable as the shadows within. Sometimes it's a sad dream—a dream sad enough to bring real tears to your sleeping eyes so that it's your tears that you wake up by, wake up to. Or again, if you're like me, there are dreams that take a turn so absurd that you wake laughing—as if you need to be awake to savor the full richness of the comedy. Rarest of all is the dream that wakes you with what I can only call its truth.

The path of your dream winds now this way, now that—one scene fades into another, people come and go the way they do in dreams—and then suddenly, deep out of wherever it is that dreams come from, something rises up that shakes you to your foundations. The mystery of the dream suddenly lifts like fog, and for an instant it is as if you glimpse a truth truer than any you knew that you knew, if only a truth about yourself. It is too much truth for the dream to hold anyway, and the dream breaks. Several years ago I had such a dream, and it is still extraordinarily fresh in my mind. I dreamt that I was staying in a hotel somewhere and that the room I was given was a room that I loved. I no longer have any clear picture of what the room looked like, and even in the dream itself I think it wasn't so much the way the room looked that pleased me as it was the way it made me feel. It was a room where I felt happy and at peace, where everything seemed the way it should be and everything about myself seemed the way it should be too. Then, as the dream went on, I wandered off to other places and did other things and finally, after many adventures, ended back at the same hotel again. Only this time I was given a different room, which I didn't feel comfortable in at all. It seemed dark and cramped, and I felt dark and cramped in it. So I made my way down to the man at the desk and told him my problem. On my earlier visit, I said, I'd had this marvelous room that was just right for me in every way and that I'd very much like if possible to have again. The trouble, I explained, was that I hadn't kept track of where the room was and didn't know how to find it or how to ask for it. The clerk was very understanding. He said that he knew exactly the room I meant and that I could have it again anytime I wanted it. All I had to do, he said, was ask for it by its name. So then, of course, I asked him what the name of the room was. He would be happy to tell me, he said, and then he told me. The name of the room, he said, was Remember.

Remember, he said. The name of the room I wanted was Remember. That was what woke me. It shocked me awake, and the shock of it, the dazzling unexpectedness of it, is vivid to me still. I knew it was a good dream, and I felt that in some unfathomable way it was also a true dream. The fact that I did not understand its truth did not keep it from being in some sense also a blessed dream, a healing dream, because you do not need to understand healing to be healed or know anything about blessing to be blessed. The sense of peace that filled me in that room, the knowledge that I could return to it whenever I wanted to or needed to-that was where the healing and blessing came from. And the name of the room—that was where the mystery came from; that was at the heart of the healing though I did not fully understand why. The name of the room was Remember. *Why* Remember? What was there about remembering that brought a peace so deep, a sense of well-being so complete and intense that it jolted me awake in my bed? It was a dream that seemed true not only for me but true for everybody. What are we to remember—all of us? To what end and purpose are we to remember?

One way or another, we are always remembering, of course. There is no escaping it even if we want to, or at least no escaping it for long, though God knows there are times when we try to, don't want to remember. In one sense the past is dead and gone, never to be repeated, over and done with, but in another sense, it is of course not done with at all or at least not done with us. Every person we have ever known, every place we have ever seen, everything that has ever happened to us—it all lives and breathes deep in us somewhere whether we like it or not, and sometimes it doesn't take much to bring it back to the surface in bits and pieces. A scrap of some song that was popular years ago. A book we read as a child. A stretch of road we used to travel. An old photograph, an old letter. There is no telling what trivial thing may do it, and then suddenly there it all is—something that happened to us once—and it is there not just as a picture on the wall to stand back from and gaze at, but as a reality we are so much a part of still and that is still so much a part of us that we feel with something close to its original intensity and freshness what it felt like, say, to fall in love at the age of sixteen, or to smell the smells and hear the sounds of a house that has long since disappeared, or to laugh till the tears ran down our cheeks with somebody who died more years ago than we can easily count or for whom, in every way that matters, we might as well have died years ago ourselves. Old failures, old hurts. Times too beautiful to tell or too terrible. Memories come at us helter-skelter and unbidden, sometimes so thick and fast that they are more than we can handle in their poignance, sometimes so sparsely that we all but cry out to remember more.

But the dream seems to say more than that, to speak of a different kind of memory and to speak of remembering in a different kind of way. The kind of memories I have been naming are memories that come and go more or less on their own and apart from any choice of ours. Things remind us, and the power is the things', not ours. The room called Remember, on the other hand, is a room we can enter whenever we like so that the power of remembering becomes our own power. Also, the kind of memories we normally have are memories that stir emotions in us that are as varied as the memories that stir them. The room called Remember, on the other hand, is a room where all emotions are caught up in and transcended by an extraordinary sense of well-being. It is the room of all rooms where we feel at home and at peace. So what do these differences point to, is the question—the difference between the haphazard memories that each day brings to us willy-nilly and the memories represented by the room in the dream?

First of all, I think, they point to remembering as much more of a conscious act of the will than it normally is for us. We are all such escape artists, you and I. We don't like to get too serious about things, especially about ourselves. When we are with other people, we are apt to talk about almost anything under the sun except for what really matters to us, except for our own lives, except for what is going on inside our own skins. We pass the time of day. We chatter. We hold each other at bay, keep our distance from each other even when God knows it is precisely each other that we desperately need.

And it is the same thing when we are alone. Let's say it is late evening and everybody else has gone away or gone to bed. The time is ripe for looking back over the day, the week, the year, and trying to figure out where we have come from and where we are going to, for sifting through the things we have done and the things we have left undone for a clue to who we are and who, for better or worse, we are becoming. But again and again we avoid the long thoughts. We turn on the television maybe. We pick up a newspaper or a book. We find some chore to do that could easily wait for the next day. We cling to the present out of wariness of the past. We cling to the surface out of fear of what lies beneath the surface. And why not, after all? We get tired. We get confused. We need such escape as we can find. But there is a deeper need yet, I think, and that is the need—not all the time, surely, but from time to time-to enter that still room within us all where the past lives on as part of the present, where the dead are alive again, where we are most alive ourselves to the long journeys of our lives with all their twistings and turnings and to where our journeys have brought us. The name of the room is Remember—the room where with patience, with charity, with quietness of heart, we remember consciously to remember the lives we have lived.

So much has happened to us all over the years. So much has happened within us and through us. We are to take time to remember what we can about it and what we dare. That's what entering the room means, I think. It means taking time to remember on purpose. It means not picking up a book for once or turning on the radio, but letting the mind journey gravely, deliberately, back through the years that have gone by but are not gone. It means a deeper, slower kind of remembering; it means remembering as a searching and finding. The room is there for all of us to enter if we choose to, and the process of entering it is not unlike the process of praying, because praying too is a slow, grave journey—a search to find the truth of our own lives at their deepest and dearest, a search to understand, to hear and be heard.

"Nobody knows the trouble I've seen" goes the old spiritual, and of course nobody knows the trouble we have any of us seen—the hurt, the sadness, the bad mistakes, the crippling losses—but we know it. We are to remember it. And the happiness we have seen too—the precious times, the precious people, the moments in our lives when we were better than we know how to be. Nobody knows that either, but we know it. We are to remember it. And then, if my dream was really a true dream, we will find, beyond any feelings of joy or regret that one by one the memories give rise to, a profound and undergirding peace, a sense that in some unfathomable way all is well.

We have survived, you and I. Maybe that is at the heart of our remembering. After twenty years, forty years, sixty years or eighty, we have made it to this year, this day. We needn't have made it. There were times we never thought we would and nearly didn't. There were times we almost hoped we wouldn't, were ready to give the whole thing up. Each must speak for himself, for herself, but I can say for myself that I have seen sorrow and pain enough to turn the heart to stone. Who hasn't? Many times I have chosen the wrong road, or the right road for the wrong reason. Many times I have loved the people I love too much for either their good or mine, and others I might have loved I have missed loving and lost. I have followed too much the devices and desires of my own heart, as the old prayer goes, yet often when my heart called out to me to be brave, to be kind, to be honest, I have not followed at all.

To remember my life is to remember countless times when I might have given up, gone under, when humanly speaking I might have gotten lost beyond the power of any to find me. But I didn't. I have not given up. And each of you, with all the memories you have and the tales you could tell, you also have not given up. You also are survivors and are here. And what does that tell us, our surviving? It tells us that weak as we are, a strength beyond our strength has pulled us through at least this far, at least to this day. Foolish as we are, a wisdom beyond our wisdom has flickered up just often enough to light us if not to the right path through the forest, at least to a path that leads forward, that is bearable. Faint of heart as we are, a love beyond our power to love has kept our hearts alive.

So in the room called Remember it is possible to find peace—the peace that comes from looking back and remembering to remember that though most of the time we failed to see it, we were never really alone. We could never have made it this far if we had had only each other to depend on, because nobody knows better than we do ourselves the undependability and frailty of even the strongest of us. Who or what was with us all those years? Who or what do we have to thank for our survival? Our lucky stars? Maybe just that. Maybe we have nothing more to thank than that. Our lucky stars.

But David the king had more than that or thought he did. "O give thanks to the Lord," he cried out, "make known his deeds among the peoples!" He had brought the ark of the covenant into Jerusalem and placed it in a room, a tent, and to the sound of harp, lyre, cymbals, and trumpet he sang his wild and exultant song. "Remember the wonderful works that he has done," he sang, "the wonders he wrought, the judgments he uttered." *Remember* was the song David sang, and what memories he had or was to have, what a life to remember! His failure as a husband and a father, his lust for Bathsheba and the murder of her husband, his crime against Naboth and the terrible denunciation of the prophet Nathan, his failures, his betrayals, his hypocrisy. But "Tell of his salvation from day to day" (1 Chron. 16:23), his song continues nonetheless and continued all his life, and I take him to mean not just that the telling was to take place from day to day, but that salvation itself takes place from day to day. Every day, as David remembered, he had been somehow saved—saved enough to survive his own darkness and lostness and folly, saved enough to go on through thick and thin to the next day and the next day's saving and the next. "Remember the wonders he wrought, the judgments he uttered," David cries out in his song, and the place where he remembers these wonders and judgments is his own past in all its brokenness and the past of his people before him, of Abraham, Isaac, and Jacob, the Exodus, the entrance into the Promised Land, which are all part of our past too as Christ also is part of our past, that Exodus, that Promised Land, and all those mightier wonders yet. That's what he remembers and sings out for us all to remember.

"Seek the Lord and his strength, seek his presence continually" goes the song—seek him in the room in the tent where the holy ark is, seek him in the room in the dream. It is the Lord, it is God, who has been with us through all our days and years whether we knew it or not, he sings with us in our best moments and in our worst moments, to heal us with his wonders, to wound us healingly with his judgments, to bless us in hidden ways though more often than not we had forgotten his name. It is God that David thanks and not his lucky stars. "O give thanks to the Lord... make known his deeds among the peoples," he sings; remember and make known the deeds that he wrought among the years of your own lives. Is he right? Was it God? Is it God we have to thank, you and I, for having made it somehow to this day?

Again each of us must speak for himself, for herself. We must, each one of us, remember our own lives. Someone died whom we loved and needed, and from somewhere something came to fill our emptiness and mend us where we were broken. Was it only time that mended, only the resurging busyness of life that filled our emptiness? In anger we said something once that we could have bitten our tongues out for afterwards, or in anger somebody said something to us. But out of somewhere forgiveness came, a bridge was rebuilt; or maybe forgiveness never came, and to this day we have found no bridge back. Is the human heart the only source of its own healing? Is it the human conscience only that whispers to us that in bitterness and estrangement is death? We listen to the evening news with its usual recital of shabbiness and horror, and God, if we believe in him at all, seems remote and powerless, a child's dream. But there are other times—often the most unexpected, unlikely times—when strong as life itself comes the sense that there is a holiness deeper than shabbiness and horror and at the very heart of darkness a light unutterable. Is it only the unpredictable fluctuations of the human spirit that we have to thank? We must each of us answer for ourselves, remember for ourselves, preach to ourselves our own sermons. But "Remember the wonderful works," sings King David, because if we remember deeply and truly, he says, we will know whom to thank, and in that room of thanksgiving and remembering there is peace.

Then hope. Then at last we see what hope is and where it comes from, hope as the driving power and outermost edge of faith. Hope stands up to its knees in the past and keeps its eyes on the future. There has never been a time past when God wasn't with us as the strength beyond our strength, the wisdom beyond our wisdom, as whatever it is in our hearts—whether we believe in God or not-that keeps us human enough at least to get by despite everything in our lives that tends to wither the heart and make us less than human. To remember the past is to see that we are here today by grace, that we have survived as a gift.

And what does that mean about the future? What do we have to hope for, you and I? Humanly speaking, we have only the human best to hope for: that we will live out our days in something like peace and the ones we love with us; that if our best dreams are never to come true, neither at least will our worst fears; that something we find to do with our lives will make some little difference for good somewhere; and that when our lives end we will be remembered a little while for the little good we did. That is our human hope. But in the room called Remember we find something beyond it.

"Remember the wonderful works that he has done," goes David's song—remember what he has done in the lives of each of us; and beyond that remember what he has done in the life of the world; remember above all what he has done in Christ—remember those moments in our own lives when with only the dullest understanding but with the sharpest longing we have glimpsed that Christ's kind of life is the only life that matters and that all other kinds of life are riddled with death; remember those moments in our lives when Christ came to us in countless disguises through people who one way or another strengthened us, comforted us, healed us, judged us, by the power of Christ alive within them. All that is the past. All that is what there is to remember. And *because* that is the past, *because* we remember, we have this high and holy hope: that what he has done, he will continue to do, that what he has begun in us and our world, he will in unimaginable ways bring to fullness and fruition.

"Let the sea roar, and all that fills it, let the field exult, and everything in it! Then shall the trees of the wood sing for joy," says David (1 Chron. 16:32-33). And *shall* is the verb of hope. Then death shall be no more, neither shall there be mourning or crying. Then shall my eyes behold him and not as a stranger. Then his Kingdom shall come at last and his will shall be done in us and through us and for us. Then the trees of the wood shall sing for joy as already they sing a little even now sometimes when the wind is in them and as underneath their singing our own hearts too already sing a little sometimes at this holy hope we have.

The past and the future. Memory and expectation. Remember and hope. Remember and wait. Wait for him whose face we all of us know because somewhere in the past we have faintly seen it, whose life we all of us thirst for because somewhere in the past we have seen it lived, have maybe even had moments of living it ourselves. Remember him who himself remembers us as he promised to remember the thief who died beside him. To have faith is to remember and wait, and to wait in hope is to have what we hope for already begin to come true in us through our hoping. Praise him.

Fiction

An Overview of Buechner's Fiction
by W. Dale Brown

Many thousands of readers have found their ways to Buechner via his nonfiction, books like *Wishful Thinking*, *Telling the Truth*, or *Alphabet of Grace*. Many others have come to Buechner via the sermon collections like *The Magnificent Defeat* or *Secrets in the Dark*. Still others have started with the memoirs: *Sacred Journey*, *Now & Then*, *Telling Secrets*, and *Eyes of the Heart*. Sure enough, there's a wealth of consolation and wisdom in Buechner's superb nonfiction. But readers would be well advised to discover the brilliant fiction, the stories and novels, alongside the collected volumes of thoughtful theology and eye-catching wit that circulate through church libraries and show up in the quips folded into sermons every week in churches all over the place.

Perhaps you know of the novel *Godric*, the story of the irascible saint, runner up for a Pulitzer Prize. The attention to that magnificent novel is well deserved. Some fans have discovered the *Bebb* books or maybe *Son of Laughter*, but allow me to commend you to the whole bunch—the 14 novels and the handful of stories—where you will discover Buechner the artist at his world class best. Frederick Buechner's characteristic themes find their deepest expression in his fiction. Attracted to the drama of Buechner's personal story? Watch the way he will weave his own personal narrative into such books as *The Wizard's Tide* and *The Final Beast*. Interested in wakefulness? Take a look at the *Bebb* stories and their encouragement to fortissimo. Appreciate Buechner's understanding of clay-footed saints? Check out *Brendan* or *The Son of Laughter*. Love those texts that reimagine biblical narratives? Read *On the Road With the Archangel*. Value Buechner's engagement with Shakespeare or Frank Baum? Check out *The Entrance to Porlock* or *The Storm*. Taken with Buechner's understanding of human anxiety and longing for meaning? Find respite in *Long Day's Dying* or *The Seasons' Difference*. Wondering about those outsized words like "integrity," and what it means to be human? Take a look at *The Return of Ansel Gibbs*. There's even an overlooked short story from the 1950's, "The Tiger," where you will get to go to a Princeton football game. Frederick Buechner's fiction embodies his gift for an intimate encounter with what we feel: the ubiquity of guilt, the elusiveness of forgiveness, the puzzle that is God, the possibility of the miraculous, and the hope that all will be well.

Buechner says that it will be the novels for which he is remembered if he is to be remembered at all. Readers who discover Buechner via the memoirs or the nonfiction often find their way to the more recent novels; some even go back to the beginning, the 1950 bestseller, *A Long Day's Dying*. Those especially curious about the development of Buechner's career will find the debut novel an important read. *A Long Day's Dying* and the second offering, the 1952 novel, *The*

Season's Difference, each are reminiscent of the age of Faulkner, Fitzgerald, and their progeny—the modernist era of fiction featuring desolation, miscommunication, and emptiness. In his earliest efforts, Buechner seems to be writing for a teacher, not yet having discovered the voice that will characterize the later work. Nonetheless, the early books offer an intriguing glimpse into the issues that will preoccupy Buechner throughout his career: guilt and grace, longing and the quest for meaning, doubt and faith.

The Return of Ansel Gibbs, Buechner's third novel, arrives in 1958 and reflects that period of Buechner's life when his work at Union Theological Seminary, his marriage, and his search for vocation come together in a book featuring a political figure puzzling over his responsibility to his country, his family, and himself. This novel reflects a somewhat freer style and makes use of material emerging from the classes at Union as well as casting an oblique look at the subject of suicide, a matter at the core of all of Buechner's writing as a consequence of his father's suicide in November of 1936.

The first two novels are sprinkled with skeptics and questions. The third novel satirizes a Bible-thumper set against a wise and quirky seminary professor with the protagonist, Ansel Gibbs, "a man of words," more or less trying to find his way to something like faith. The fourth novel, *The Final Beast*, marks a turn in the career as it comes after Buechner's ordination to the Presbyterian ministry and his years of work as a teacher of Religious Studies at Phillip's Exeter Academy. *The Final Beast* contains the fullest expression of the ideas echoing softly through the first three novels and resounding through the later work; it is thus a pivotal book in the Buechner canon.

The novel centers on a dazed young clergyman. His wife dead in a senseless accident, Theodore Nicolet must persevere for the sake of his two young children. In spite of the cloud of bafflement hanging over the remnant of his family, he must continue to minister to his congregation in a New England village. Nicolet works his way through perplexity about God, his calling to the ministry, his distant father, and his troubled parishioners. Readers will find here that Buechnerian voice that resounds in later work, the voice preoccupied with matters of forgiveness and guilt, passion and wakefulness. His theological studies and his ordination have provided a base, a confidence, which emerges in this book in both its theme and its comfortable style. Buechner often jokes that the ministry was a bad career move for a writer, and some critics pounced on the tenuous union between clergyman and novelist when *The Final Beast* appeared in 1965. This is a good starting place among Buechner's novels as it is a curiously dark novel about joy, an early formulation of Buechner's theory of the interplay of tragedy, comedy, and fairy tale.

The fairy tale theme will continue into Buechner's 1970 novel, *The Entrance to Porlock,* as Buechner weaves a fiction making use of Frank Baum's *Wizard of Oz.* Perhaps Buechner's most neglected book, this novel appears at a moment of great turmoil in the country. Buechner struggled with the novel, even calling it a "strangled book," one "born by Caesarian Section." Nonetheless, readers will find here a continuing preoccupation with the possibility of authentic religious experience even as

Buechner stays far away from the stained glass this time. In reaction to those critics who responded with alarm at the religious dimensions of *The Final Beast*, Buechner keeps the religious at arm's length in *The Entrance to Porlock*. The only sermon is something about paying attention, and the only conclusions circle on the long-shot possibility of quenching those deepest, inexpressible human longings. This is a cloudy book replete with Buechnerian shadow. In this fifth novel, Buechner does, however, reiterate his belief that reality, though puzzling and difficult, is fraught with meaning, and he continues the premise into the *Bebb* tetralogy that will occupy him for most of the 1970's.

If *Porlock* is a parable, then the raucous *Bebb* novels tumbling out from 1971-1977, register another pivotal moment in Buechner's career as he moves further from the restrained literary style of the earlier novels to a sometimes bawdy, often humorous, and rapidly moving prose in the *Bebb* books. The four novels tell one periodic tale of Antonio Parr's involvement in the life of Leo Bebb, itinerant preacher, diploma salesman, ex-convict, saint, and/or hypocrite. Although Antonio Parr narrates the stories, and the reader sees through Antonio's eyes, Bebb broods over the narrative throughout. Because Leo Bebb is, ostensibly, a man of the cloth, Buechner can comfortably interweave religious rhetoric, biblical allusions, and theological considerations as he has in *The Final Beast*. Bebb is anything but a typical clergyman, however, and *The Book of Bebb* emphatically is not a collection of religious novels. The novels are religious only in their implications and suggestions, never directly. Theodore Nicolet, despite his introspection and doubt, is a staunchly orthodox minister beside Leo Bebb, the colorful and controversial preacher of the tetralogy. They both wear robes when they preach, but the comparison stops there.

The Book of Bebb continues with the questions dominating all of Buechner's work: belief versus unbelief, the ambiguities of life, the nature of sin, human lostness, spiritual homesickness, the quest for self-identity, the need for self-revelation, the search for meaning, and the possibility of joy. God is argued for and argued against in these books, but he is never absent. Buechner refuses to smuggle in a conventional religious conclusion; he simply reports, instead, a faith struggle—a delicately balanced statement of affirmation and doubt. The first-person *Bebb* novels allow Buechner room for an entertaining voice that is somewhat new to his fiction. Although many of the usual questions remain in these books of the 1970's, we see Buechner discovering the theme that he will hone in subsequent decades: clay-footed heroes, unwitting saints.

Buechner refers to the writing of *Bebb* as a "love affair"; the book that follows in 1980, *Godric*, will be simply called "a blessing." It is the book that Buechner hopes to be remembered by and clearly establishes a pinnacle point among his many achievements. The fictionalized version of the historical Saint Godric was to garner a runner-up nomination for a Pulitzer Prize as well as plaudits from both sides of the secular/religious critical debate. Coming at this novel for the first time, readers may discover a challenge. The language is twelfth century, the style is poetic, and the time scheme is anything but chronological. Nonetheless, *Godric* is one of those books which become significant markers along the way. The plot line is simple enough: a young monk, Reginald, has been commissioned to write the story of a venerated hermit, Godric. Much of the novel circles on which version of events we are to believe.

Are we to trust in Reginald, the official biographer? Or should we believe Godric, the one who lived the life after all? Or is there a third version that we intuit for ourselves, a story suspended in the space between the two accounts recorded in the novel, Buechner's version, perhaps? As it turns out, "nothing human's not a broth of false and true," as Godric puts it. In memorable prose, Buechner fastens on the problem of truth, realizes that any story has many versions; all perspectives are limited and partial. The tension of the novel, then, fixes on the expurgated saint's life Reginald is writing and Godric's own earthy and guilt-ridden story.

When Reginald, for example, parses the meaning of "Godric" as Saxon for "God's reign," Godric argues that "ric" is Erse for "wreck;" thus his name signifies "God's wreck." He explains, "God's wreck I be, it means. God's wrecked Godric for his sins. Or Godric's sins have made a wreck of God." *Godric* is a miracle for Buechner, and in bringing the venerable saint alive for himself, Buechner brings him alive for readers as well. *Godric* has assured him a larger audience and discovery by a new generation of readers. The novel is showing up on college syllabi and being listed with the great books of our time. His place as a novelist of consequence is settled with *Godric*. The tension between belief and unbelief, between hope and despair—the heart of Buechner's work—will endure as the vital center of his career.

Seven years later after a turn toward memoir and nonfiction, Buechner returns to the themes of *Godric* in his eleventh novel, *Brendan*. Apparently, there really was a Brendan. According to Buechner's historical note, the man was born in 484 in what is now Tralee, Ireland, and died ninety-four years later at Anaghdown, Ireland. Brendan's adventures turn up primarily in *Navigatio Sancti Brendani*, a tenth-century version of his life that had wide popularity for its medieval lore and was translated into many languages. Educated by Bishop Erc and Saint Jarlath, Brendan became a builder of monasteries as well as an evangelist for the new faith. He helped establish one of Ireland's first Christian kings, Hugh the Handsome, and converted the pagan bard, MacLennin, who eventually becomes a saint himself. But Brendan's primary fame derives from his voyages in search of Tir-na-n-Og, the Celtic otherworld, an imagined paradise. According to the legends, Brendan may have sailed as far as Florida in his questing after the place of peace. In any case, his many journeys as a bard for Christ make perfect material for a picaresque depiction of medieval cultural conflicts and human longings. The missionary, Brendan, is living off the seed sown by Saint Patrick a generation or so before. While Europe is still dark, Ireland is alive with the new faith, but the old gods are not finished just yet. Buechner takes the conversion of Ireland and Wales as his subject, the book growing from a scene he imagines, a moment of great violence, where Brendan brings down his club on a fertility idol. Playing like a film in his imagination, that germ leads Buechner to find his way beyond Brendan's history and into his inner life.

Like most of Buechner's heroes, Brendan gets everything wrong and yet, somehow, gets the one big thing right. Given a few pages to focus *Brendan* in the memoir *Telling Secrets*, Buechner goes to the scene where Finn and Brendan realize that

Gildas the Wise has only one leg. "I'm as crippled as the dark world," Gildas confesses. "If it comes to that, which one of us isn't, my dear?" Brendan answers. Thus Buechner reads his own book as underscoring incompleteness and need. But he also adds something of the lesson Brendan is slow to learn. "'The kingdom of God is among you,' Jesus said—the Land of the Blessed... It is not beyond the western horizon that the Kingdom lies but among you, among ourselves, within ourselves and our life together," Buechner writes. *Brendan* is a novel, finally, about misunderstanding. And the one most misunderstood is one who moves only dimly in the background—God himself. The wind of this theme will fill Buechner's sails now for voyages into the Old Testament with *The Son of Laughter* in 1993 and into the Apocryphal book *Tobit* for the 1997 novel, *On the Road with the Archangel*.

The trouble with Bible stories, of course, is that we've already heard them, heard them so often that we've stopped listening. In the early 1990's Buechner decides to take on Genesis, tell us a tale we already know. *The Son of Laughter* is the story of the biblical patriarch Jacob, a man we thought we knew. We've seen the paintings that celebrate his midnight struggle with an angel. We remember the humor and the horror of those years he spent fruitlessly laboring for the wrong wife. We've probably seen flannel board versions of the famous coat of many colors that, to his regret, he gave to a favorite son. We've read about the tricks that he played on others and the tricks that were played on him. Buechner has become fascinated with saints who are also scoundrels. Buechner finds his way into the gaps of the Jacob-record in much the same way that he had imagined his way into the lesser known histories of Godric and Brendan. He breathes new vitality into familiar stories this time, managing to find remarkable relevance in those tales we've heard from childhood. *The Son of Laughter* is yet another departure, the surprise this time in how Buechner makes Jacob's story our own.

Past the age of 70 in the late 1990's and thinking about the sort of work that might summarize his career, Buechner surprises yet again with *On the Road with the Archangel*, a novel with a dramatically fairy tale quality, a lightness that seems a break from the three preceding novels. The original *Tobit* was probably excluded from the sixty-six book biblical canon because of its folktale quality, and Buechner manages to exploit the fun of the genre even in the muddle of Job-like questions and situations. Job's questions are Tobit's indeed—Who is this Jehovah? and Why is this happening to me? This novel is Buechner's happiest, despite plenty enough ugliness to go around. Tobit is a faithful enough fellow, but he has completely misunderstood Jehovah, whom he calls "the scorekeeper."

This terse novel is simply a good story. It would be unfortunate to overlook it because of its brevity and fairy tale dimension. *On the Road with the Archangel* is another of those animations of old stories we've filed away. In our contemporary penchant for thrillers and soon-to-be-a-movie blockbusters, little books like this one are easily missed. Through these ancient characters, Buechner raises the familiar questions of belief and unbelief. The real-life questions that Buechner has a penchant for turn up here again and again: the emptiness of a household where the children have departed into their own lives, the problem of the poverty and pain of so many, the honesty of unbelief, and the terror of faith. Finally, *On the Road with the Archangel* centers on the question of whether or not there is really a Holy One who looks after the world. Answering "NO" is understandable enough, Buechner understands. He reminds us, nonetheless, that expecting the worst is easy, but sometimes the best is there for those with eyes to see. Maybe "yes" is the last word after all. Maybe even "YES."

And finally comes *The Storm*, Buechner's turn to "The Tempest," Shakespeare's own late career masterpiece. Kenzie Maxwell is Buechner's protagonist here, another of those troubled and complicated Buechner types. He's been married twice before marrying his third wife, Willow. Maybe he has simply married her for her money and/or social status. And their arrangement is complicated by hints of a scandal hanging in the background. The plot of *The Storm* is driven by Kenzie's disreputable past, a life sidetracked by a sordid affair that has threatened to crush him into nothingness. Once a promising writer, Kenzie now carries a "burden of sadness and shame and loss that lay beneath everything he did to conceal it." Kenzie's guilt is a troublesome load not unlike the burden old Godric had to bear. The story is itself is quickly told as tragedies often are. A scandalous affair has ended with the death of his lover, Kia; but the child of their forbidden love-making is real enough. Buechner moves abruptly to the consequences. Left with a daughter, Bree, Kenzie must try to find a way to navigate both the sorrow and the scandal. For twenty years, Kenzie has tried to take care of Bree while writing a rambling journal to Kia, the waif he cannot forget, the love he cannot decipher.

It is this mixed and mixed-up man whose story Buechner tells in a third-person narrative this time. Like Bebb before him, who with Kenzie proclaims, "I believe everything" and like Buechner himself, who admits, "I am a hopelessly religious person," Kenzie is moved by things he cannot see. None of them ever declares that such belief is easy, however. Readers will discover here another study of dysfunctional families and the specter of the endearing sinner, themes that Buechner has turned to repeatedly. The driving idea this time is mercy, forgiveness. Will Kenzie Maxwell recover from his disgraceful plummet? Will he forgive others? Will he forgive himself?

Thus the novels summarize the career. From *A Long Day's Dying* to *The Final Beast,* from the *Bebb* books to *The Storm,* Buechner has attempted to write novels that embrace questions of faith. He manages to discuss religious ideas—grace, sin, and spiritual longing—without becoming didactic, preachy, or one-dimensional. Readers often find their way into the work of Frederick Buechner via a dizzying array of avenues. Rather surprisingly, Buechner says that the novels have been the locus of his most personal, most overt, perspective on his intuitions about faith in God. But there are also the collections of essays, the memoirs, and even a couple of short stories that offer other points of entry into Buechner's long and multifaceted career. Some of Buechner's work is remarkably difficult to classify. In this brief survey of the novels, I have omitted, for example, the 1990 book, *The Wizard's Tide.* This short volume, first marketed as a children's book, is a fictionalized account of Buechner's youth and the dramatic events surrounding his father's suicide. The book sits easily beside *The Sacred Journey* and probably is best located among the memoirs. Trying to decide where to start with Buechner is probably a matter of taste as much as anything else, but the novels remain the skeletal material on which the volumes of nonfiction and autobiographical works are arranged.

Because he offers that rare combination of literary artist and creative believer who speaks to our longing to believe as well as to our inescapable doubts, Buechner's audience has blossomed. Buechner has continued to offer an unblinking encounter, which, I suspect, is what we most want in those books we keep around. The best summary is probably located in Godric's voice, his last words: "All's lost. All's found." The four words pose the Buechnerian balance, the trembling tension, in which readers are finding significant consolation and, in some instances, even a way toward faith.

Excerpts from *Godric*

Of Godric, his friends, and Reginald.

FIVE friends I had, and two of them snakes. Tune and Fairweather they were, thick round as a man's arm, my bedmates and playfellows, keepers of my skimped hearth and hermit's heart till in a grim pet I bade them go that day and nevermore to come again, nevermore to hiss their snakelove when they saw me drawing near or coil themselves for warmth about my shaggy legs. They went. They never came again.

I spied them now and then, puddling my way home like a drowned man from dark Wear with my ballocks shriveled to beansize in their sack and old One-eye scarce a barnacle's length clear of my belly and crying a-mercy. It was him as I sought in freezing Wear to teach a lesson that he never learned nor has to this day learned though wiser, you'd think, for sixty winters' dunking in bonechilling, treacherous Wear. Not him. I would spy my gentle Tune and watchdog, firetooth Fairweather watching me as still as death in the long grass or under a stone as I hied home sodden on cracked feet, but none of us ever let on that we were seeing what we saw until we saw no longer. I miss them no more or hardly do, past most such sweet grieving now at age above a hundred if I've got time straight for once. For old Godric's now more dead than quick, a pile of dark rags left to steam and scorch now by the fire. It's the missing them now I miss.

That's two. The third was Roger Mouse, as stout of heart and limb as foul of mouth, plowing the stormy seas for pilfer or prize. He had an eye out ever for the willing maids, and no matter to Mouse were they flaxen locked Dane or black Spaniard, old as earth or cherryripe for the plucking. No matter to Mouse if the deck was awash and storm in the rigging. He'd play with them at diddelydum the weather be damned and cared not a pin that the eyes of the oars were upon them. What a man was Mouse! What a sinner too was Mouse, but none was ever a fonder friend, and what with all the man's great mirth, there was less room left in him for truly mortal sin than in your landlocked, penny-pinching chapmen working their cheerless stealth at the fairs where we peddled.

We had rabbitfur, goosefeather, beeswax, calfskin, garlic and gauds galore. We'd load them cheap the one place and unload them dear the other for any fatrump mistress or dungfoot pilgrim with cockles in his hat that had the pence to squander. We grew rich till one fine day the *Saint Esprit* was ours with her sharp prow that sliced the waves like cheese. Mouse stood so high he said it blew the caps off men who stood astern when he broke wind. Godric was captain helmsman with a canny nose for weather, and captain Mouse was Godric's charm against the Evil Eye, for, mark you, Mouse's sin smacked less of evil than of larkishness the likes of which Our Lord himself could hardly help but wink at when he spied it out in whore and prodigal.

I loved Mouse. Together we saved a Christian king from infidels and not a silver coin to split between us for our pains. Years afterward, two hundred miles and more away in my dry hut, I saw Mouse in the eye of my heart go down with *Saint Esprit* off the Welsh rocks. He cried out the only name he knew me by, which was not Godric, and in the ear of my heart I heard him, helpless.

Ailred was fourth. They say as a babe he reared up like a lily in his tub and spoke the *Pater Noster* through nor would take of his mother's teat for the forty days and nights of Lent save Sabbaths. He grew to a sheaf of bones made fast round the middle with a monk's rope.

The pictish king of Galloway was the devil fleshed. He had the gold eyes of a toad and a forked beard. On cold nights he'd slit a slave's belly open like a sack so he could dabble his feet in the warm bowels. He tied together the limbs of women in labor for sport and drank blood. Ailred went to him. Throned on a rock, the king was picking his teeth with the bone of a weasel when Ailred knelt and watered his shins with tears. They say a light went forth from Ailred then that blinded the king's gold eyes, and a creature was seen passing forth out of the king hung all over with bottles of the blood he'd drunk, and the king swore holy faith from that day on and took him the name of Ailred for his own. Thus with no loss of seed or purity, my friend got him a son that day upon the rock, and Jesu a forkbeard, pictish knight though blind as a bat from that day on.

Ailred himself they made abbot after a time at Rievaulx where so great was his meekness the fat monks vied with each other to try it till one day one of them, finding him flat in a swoon from an attack of the stone, plucked him up as weighed no more than the weight of his thin bones and cast him onto the fire. But Ailred forgave him, wouldn't you know. He'd let them harm no hair of the monk's head for the mischief he'd done. Nor was Ailred himself so much as singed.

He visits me from time to time. You'd never take him for holy. He smells of fish, his smock hiked up to his hips and his long legs lank as a heron's as he picks his way along the banks of Wear coughing his fearsome cough.

"Peace, Godric," he says.

He's all bones. Godric's all rags. They kneel there hours on end under the low thatch without a word to clutter the silence save for the prayers they heave heavenward braided together like a hawser the better to hoist the world a cat's whisker out of the muck. Only once did he do me a bad turn, and that was from love as many a bad turn's been done from before. He sent me Reginald.

"To put your life on parchment, Godric," Ailred says. His cough's like the splitting of wood. "To unbushel the light of your days for the schooling of children. To set them a path to follow." Did he but know where Godric's path has led or what sights his light has lit, he'd bushel me back fast enough. I've told Mother Reginald tales to rattle his beads and blush his fishbelly tonsure pink as a babe's bum, but he turns them all to treacle with his scratching quill. I scoop out the jakes of my remembrance, and he censes it all with his clerkish screed till it reeks of mass. He brings me broth and plovers' eggs. He freshens my straw when I foul it. If some dream shipwrecks me at night, he's there with his taper to beacon me safe to shore. Just the sight of his sheepface gives me the cramp.

I lie with my eyes rolled back to the whites and my jaws agape so he'll think I'm a corpse before he's dug his book from me. Often I speak to him only with the tongue of my hands which he does not understand. I have taught rats to run over him in the dark. But I suffer him. For it was lowly, gentle, dark-eyed Ailred sent him.

The fifth was Gillian. I met her on a Roman hill with Aedwen, my mother, drowsing at my side. She journeyed in our pilgrim band. At each day's end she'd bathe my feet. She crept beneath my cloak.

I have forgotten my father's face. I have forgotten my own face when I was young. By God's mercy someday I will forget Reginald's face. But her face I'll remember ever. Gillian I will not forget.

That's five friends, one for each of Jesu's wounds, and Godric bears their mark still on what's left of him as in their time they all bore his on them. What's friendship, when all's done, but the giving and taking of wounds?

When Godric banished Fairweather and Tune, they all three bled for it, and part of Godric snaked off too nevermore to come again. And it's Godric's flesh that Ailred's cough cleaves like an axe. And when brave Mouse went down off Wales, he bore to the bottom the cut of Godric's sharp farewell. And when Gillian vanished in a Dover wood, she took with her all but the husk of Godric's joy.

Gentle Jesu, Mary's son, be thine the wounds that heal our wounding. Press thy bloody scars to ours that thy dear blood may flow in us and cleanse our sin.

Be thou in us and we in thee that Godric, Gillian, Ailred, Mouse and thou may be a woundless one at last. And even Reginald if thy great mercy reach so far.

137

In God's name Godric prays. Amen.

How Godric met a boar and a leper and
how people sought him in his cell.

I can no longer hold my water and itch in places I haven't scratched these twenty years for the clownish stiffness in my bones. It's Reginald that has to swab my bum and deems the task a means of grace. I've got an old dam's dugs. My privities hang loose as poultry from a hook. My head wags to and fro. There's times my speech comes out so thick and gobbled I'd as well to save my wind. But the jest is bitterer yet, for deep inside this wrecked and ravaged hull, there sails a young man still.

How I rage at times to smite with these same fists I scarce can clench! How I long, when woods are green, to lark and leap on shanks grown dry as sticks! Let a maid but pass my way with sport in her eye and her braid a-swinging, and I burn for her although my wick's long since burnt out and in my heart's eye see her as the elders saw Susanna at her bath—her belly pale and soft as whey, her pippins, her slender limbs and thistledown. So ever and again young Godric's dreams well up to flood old Godric's prayers, or prayers and dreams reach God in such a snarl he has to comb the tangle out, and who knows which he counts more dear.

Is he asleep, old Godric? Is he awake? Does he himself know which? He lies there staring at a crack. He mumbles holiness. They say he first saw light in Bastard William's day, and now it's Henry Second, Becket's bane, that calls the tune from France.

They say that Godric's body's scored from when the Devil, shaped like a wild boar, fetched him down and tore him. They say he healed a leper with a kiss. They kneel there waiting for him to rise or stir while Godric mocks them in his peacock heart.

What can such whispering gawkers know of hot, foul breath, he thinks, of slobbered tusks and eyes like coals? Fierce from a thicket it sprang on him with snuffling rage, but Godric knew it for the Prince of Darkness by the golden circlet on its brow and signed it with the cross. From snout and pizzle blood spewed forth. Then, as it screamed, its maw filled up with flames till there was nothing left of it except a stench so vile that Godric swooned.

And let them say what cost the kiss I gave one rainy day on Dover Road.

I see the shape approaching still. Its clothes are patched with white and on its head a tall red hat all bent and faded pale from years of weather. *Frick-frack, frick-frack* its rattle goes, and as I climb the bank to let it pass, the very mist shrinks back to flee its touch. The mire is gullied deep, and as it nears my perch, it trips and topples to the ground. It tries to rise but flounders down again. It whimpers like a child that's being flogged. The rain is pelting hard, and flat on its belly in the muck it might well drown for all I know. So less from pity than from fear to have a murder on my soul, I go to help it to its feet. As I bend down, it turns to face me. Then I see it has no face.

I can't say if it was a man I kissed or maid or why I kissed at all. I've seen them make the sick eat broth by holding it so close the savor draws them on. Maybe misery has a savor too so if you're near enough, sick though you be with sin, your heart can't help but sup. In any case, I closed my eyes against that foul and ashen thing that once was human flesh like mine and kissed its pain. When it reached out to me, I fled till I was far enough away to puke my loathing in a ditch.

The tale they tell is of a leper cleansed. I do not know nor seek to know, for pride lies one way, rue the other. But from that time the word went forth that there was healing in my hands. *Something* was in my hands at least and rests there yet though they're all knotted now and stiff like claws. Folk come from miles to have me touch them. Could I but touch the churlishness within myself or kiss old Godric clean!

Here's how it happens when they come. They go to the monks at Durham first. "Where be the way to the hermit?" they ask. They say, "We're here to see the one as cools his holy bum in Wear come sun or snow." "To what end see him?" ask the monks, for to some I could be just as well a hanging or a calf that's got two heads. Others would sell me fowl, or have me bless some trinket, or take a snippet of my beard back home to keep off warts. And some there are who come to try me if they can.

I remember a plump maid once with apples in her cheeks and drooping lids. She'd finished telling all her fleshly sins and knelt for shriving when all at once she flung her clothes above her head and nimble as a tumbler at a fair went topsy-turvy with her bum aloft. I had my own sport then. Tune was sleeping in his jar but at my call shot forth and lunged at her. Hey nonny nonny off she went then! Nor did she stop, I'll vow, till Orkney rocks.

The monks do the sieving, as I say, and send to Godric only those deemed worthy, though I'd guess that if a gallows rat should slip a coin into their cowls, they'd send him too. And to each they give a cross of plaited straw to be his proof they've sent him. Else Reginald will drive them off.

To touch me and to feel my touch they come. To take at my hands whatever of Christ or comfort such hands have. Of their own, my hands have nothing more than any man's and less now at this tottering, lamewit age of mine when most of what I ever had is more than mostly spent. But it's as if my hands are gloves, and in them other hands than mine, and those the ones that folk appear with roods of straw to seek. It's holiness they hunger for, and if by some mad grace it's mine to give, if I've a holy hand inside my hand to touch them with, I'll touch them day and night. Sweet Christ, what other use are idle hermits for?

But then from time to time a day will dawn when suddenly my blood runs chill for thinking that what holiness I have is mine to *keep* lest, losing it, I lose the hand within my hand, my own heart's heart, my own life's life. And then I fend them off like leeches come to suck my blood. Reginald lets them in. I scowl at them. Or will not speak. Or feign some fatal ill or sleep.

Or sometimes, fierce with rage, I'll even crouch on hands and knees and shake my hair and beard into a snarl and roar at them. And sometimes even then, so great their need, they'll risk their skins by kneeling down to kiss me as they might a leper.

How Godric became Deric and sailed the
seas with Roger Mouse.

WE stood on the deck of *Saint Esprit*, myself and Mouse. She was running free before a wind that shook our beards, and Mouse kept his cap pulled down about his ears. He had his arm around my shoulder and smelled of onions. Once in a while the sea would crest, but mostly it was great blue hills with foam for heather. A swell would rise and glitter in the sun, then slide and sink into a dale. A dale would heave into a hill.

"The waves are like the years the way they meld" Mouse called against the wind. "Great Alfred's arse, while yet we can, we better ... " and then when a gust blew off his nether words, he sang it out for fair. "LIVE! LIVE!" he cried. And such was Mouse. He lived and gave me lessons in the art.

He called me by the name I'd told him there at Farne. Gudericus, I said, when asked. He said it was too much to mouth and chopped it down to Deric. So Deric I was to him from that day forth, nor did he ever know of Godric. Why did I play him false like that? I think in some way it was Cuthbert's doing. "Do good," he bade me. He laid that holy charge on Godric's head. But goodness was not Godric's meat. Wealth was he after and sport and hazard, so rather than deny the old saint's bidding, he denied his proper name instead.

The boat Mouse sailed me in to Farne did not belong to him but to a Newcastle shipwright by the name of Curran that he let her from. Curran was growing dim of wit with age so it took no greater trick to gull him of his craft than the leaky tale of how we'd lost her in a squall that splintered her against the rocks. A broad-beamed, lumpish thing she was, forever thumped by every wave, but we hugged the shore with her, and she served us for a year or two of seaborne sharping. We hauled fish in her, wool and hides. We put in at fairs. What we picked up from the dullard Scots for groats we'd peddle off for pence from Yarmouth south to Ramsgate, then turn back and try to fill our purse the other way. Here or there we'd hire louts to help with loading, then keep them on as crew until the time came round to pay them for their pains. When that day dawned, we'd go ashore and in some pothouse ply them so with beer their brains were all awash, then leave them there to wonder when they waked if Mouse and Deric both were nothing but a dream.

One of these, a rogue named Colin we'd already gulled some months before, we chanced upon again inside a Portsmouth stews. Mouse had a meaty wench with painted pippins and I a wall-eyed beauty with one hand lopped off for thieving when Colin came clomping in and spotted us. It was fox and geese then down the lane, and Colin with a wicked blade and Mouse and I as bare as birth, our goosenecks flapping. Thanks be to God we somehow got away and cast off before he sniffed us out again. And so it ever was, for from the start my Mouse and I had luck.

We traded Curran's tub for shares in other craft, each fleeter and stouter than the last, and each time cast our cozening peddlers' nets still wider yet till we were catching gulls and boobies as far afield as Flanders, Denmark, France. And thus we saw the world, did Mouse and Deric, as also did the world see us. I won't say either side was better for the sight, but ah, what times we had! Such romps and routs and carefree sinning that if we'd died, unshriven as we were, we'd both be dangling now on red-hot hooks in Hell. What's more we soon grew rich as well. By the time that I was thirty-odd and Mouse's beard already showed a sprig or two of grey, we owned each one a moiety of the *Saint Esprit*. She had a red sail and a high, sharp prow and a proper crew by then that we paid proper wages.

And after a time, along with all our hides and fish, we took to stowing pilgrims too.

From Bristol we'd haul them to Santiago de Compostela in seven days and back in five with the wind our way. They'd gather on the shore all swaddled in their shaggy robes and round felt hats, armed with their staffs and bedding and bottles. A priest would bless their setting forth. He even threw another blessing in for free to cover both the *Saint Esprit* and Mouse and me. We'd load them then. The old and sick we'd swing aboard with ropes, the rest would clamber on the best they could with the freshening breeze to toss the women's skirts on high, and how the crew would squint and crane to see what they could see. They were Venetian seamen mostly, as brown and spry as apes, and naked save for clouts to hide their lechery. As the anchor was weighed, a pilgrim often leapt upon a barrel at the mast and with a cross clutched to his breast would lead them in a parting psalm. "Had not the Lord been on our side, the proudful waters would have swamped our souls," he'd chant when we put out. Months later when we moored again, "Praise to the good Christ and Virgin kind." In between they'd leave their sins with good Saint James in Spain and also, if their luck was lean, their pence and chattels in the holds of pirates.

Many times we were boarded and sacked. It happened most at night, and often they were merchant seamen like ourselves instead of true sea-robbers. They'd draw along as if for news or succor, and the next we knew, they'd have their grapples out. Sometimes they wouldn't stop at honest thieving either but would take some poor folk off to sell as slaves. At Narbonne, on the coast of France, they say a pair of Christian souls that Jesus died to save would buy a mule. Mouse and Deric they'd bind fast with ropes so there was nothing we could do but lie there gasping on the deck like fish.

Deric it was who, shame to say, from master villains such as these learned how to work some villainy of his own. Before the *Saint Esprit* put off, he'd hide himself aboard so not a pilgrim ever saw his face. Then when they were several days from shore and it was night, he'd grime his face and knot his hair and with a handful of the crew would man the cockboat that we towed astern. Then he'd have them row around amidships where the pilgrims slept, throw up a ladder, and therewith lead his men aboard with daggers clenched between their teeth and howling like a pack of fiends from Hell. "Help! Pirates! Help!" the pilgrims cried.

To dupe them further, Deric and his men would lash Mouse to the mast where he would feign to curse and threaten while they shook each pilgrim like a sack until the last few groats came tumbling out. Then over the side into the cock again to split with Mouse some later time, nor any pilgrim ever saw the ruse.

Sometimes Mouse would play the pirate's part and Deric let himself be bound, and then they'd play the gammon out the same except that Mouse found pence less sweet than certain other fruit. Right there beneath the stars, in sight of God and man, I've seen him so caught up in tumbling pilgrim maids he'd clean forget the other treasure he was there to take. One time my anger grew so hot I broke my bonds and doused him with a pail of chill, grey sea. But Mouse was plunged so deep into his work, I think he never even knew.

Nonetheless our fights were few those first, far days. We loved each other, Mouse and I, and our love was born of need, for so it always is with mortal folk. God's love's all gift, for God has need of naught, but human folk love one another for the way they fill each other's emptiness. I needed Mouse for his strength and mirth and daring. Mouse needed me for my mettle and my wit. Even when the stars were mostly hid, I knew to plot a course by stars, and my parrot beak was ever keen to peck the weather's secret out. I could sniff a gale some three days off, and though we voyaged leagues away from home, I always knew when rain came trickling through my father's thatch or when the sun shone bright on Burcwen's hair.

Such was Godric's roistering at sea. His neck grew thick. His chest grew deep. His beard bloomed to a wild black bush. His wealth piled up like dung. He feared God little, men still less. He wenched and broiled. He peddled, gulled and stole. He helmed the *Saint Esprit* through many a black and windy sea. And yet. And yet. In the midst of all those stormy times there were moments too of calm when every now and then he'd set his sails again for Farne.

The holy isle would rise with pinnacles and sheer, grey cliffs all laden soft with birds. Her air was white with wings. Her silence broken only by their cries. Her winds were chill and sweet with salt.

I'd scale ashore and find the fish-shaped rock. I'd dig down with a spade so I'd be sure my trove was safe, then lay with it whatever more I had while Mouse kept watch on deck below. He'd tell the crew the lie I first told him, how I was there for penance for my sins. Thus if they chanced to spy me kneeling at my work, perhaps they even thought he told the truth. Who knows? In some way deeper than he knew, perhaps he did.

Once I thought I saw Saint Cuthbert's hare. He was crouched above me on the ledge, but when I called to him, he fled. And once I thought I saw the holy saint himself.

I was scattering pebbles on the fresh-turned soil to hide my tracks, my fingers stiff with cold, when something caused the birds to fear. A host of them rose up and filled the air. They creaked and swirled and scattered down, and it was in their midst I thought I saw him stand. His beard and cloak were white as they. He was leaning on a stick as if he'd traveled far. I thought his face was full of grief.

I reached my hands to him, but when I moved, the birds flew off, unfurled above the water like a flag. Where they had been, there was no more to see but only heather and a pile of stones. I knelt there till my beard froze stiff with tears.

Of Wear and Perkin and Godric's tomb.

HERE are the sounds of Wear. It rattles stone on stone. It sucks its teeth. It sings. It hisses like the rain. It roars. It laughs. It claps its hands. Sometimes I think it prays. In winter, through the ice, I've seen it moving swift and black as Tune, without a sound.

Here are the sights of Wear. It falls in braids. It parts at rocks and tumbles round them white as down or flashes over them in silver quilts. It tosses fallen trees like bits of straw yet spins a single leaf as gentle as a maid. Sometimes it coils for rest in darkling pools and sometimes leaps its banks and shatters in the air. In autumn I've seen it breathe a mist so thick and grey you'd never know old Wear was there at all.

Each day, for years and years, I've gone and sat in it. Usually at dusk I clamber down and slowly sink myself to where it laps against my breast. Is it too much to say, in winter, that I die? Something of me dies at least.

First there's the fiery sting of cold that almost stops my breath, the aching torment in my limbs. I think I may go mad, my wits so outraged that they seek to flee my skull like rats a ship that's going down. I puff. I gasp. Then inch by inch a blessed numbness comes. I have no legs, no arms. My very heart grows still. These floating hands are not my hands. The ancient flesh I wear is rags for all I feel of it.

"Praise, praise!" I croak. Praise God for all that's holy, cold, and dark. Praise him for all we lose, for all the river of the years bears off. Praise him for stillness in the wake of pain. Praise him for emptiness. And as you race to spill into the sea, praise him yourself, old Wear. Praise him for dying and the peace of death.

In the little church I built of wood for Mary, I hollowed out a place for him. Perkin brings him by the pail and pours him in. Now that I can hardly walk, I crawl to meet him there. He takes me in his chilly lap to wash me of my sins. Or I kneel down beside him till within his depths I see a star.

Sometimes this star is still. Sometimes she dances. She is Mary's star. Within that little pool of Wear she winks at me. I wink at her. The secret that we share I cannot tell in full. But this much I will tell. What's lost is nothing to what's found, and all the death that ever was, set next to life, would scarcely fill a cup.

It's where I baptised Perkin too. Perkin's not a friend, and hence I did not name him with the five. Ailred. Mouse. The snakes. And Gillian even. What made them friends was this.

Fancy us each perched on a different rock in Wear. The water races in between with strength enough to kill. But each of us reached out to touch the other, and our friendship was the comfort of that touch.

With Perkin, it is something else. Instead of standing on a different rock from mine, he is the rock I stand on as perhaps in some way I am also his. I never got a maid with child, or if I did, I never heard. So Perkin is the son I never had.

He's a saucy lad, green-eyed and ruddy-cheeked and fair. He has no special wit with words. His clothes need washing, and his hair's a snarl. He tries to grow a beard, but all that sprouts is thistledown. Often he makes sport of me. He apes my limp and goes *gub gub* to show me how I stammer when I'm overwrought. He doesn't give a whit for holy church, and when I have him kneel for blessing as he goes, he rolls his eyes at me and gapes. Yet how to tell the fathoms that I feel?

Now that I've traveled all these leagues from birth with just an inch or two to creep till death, Perkin is the years I'll never see, and thus my son. But he's the hands that bring me food and drink as well, the arm I need to walk, the lips that teach me cheer, and thus he is my father too.

He helped me make my tomb. He was only a lad of ten or so and I still able then to wield a mallet. I found a great square stone as hard as flint to last. Week after week we pounded it and scraped. We chiseled deep and polished as we went. We never lost a thumb like Ralph the mason, but many a nail turned black from where the mallet missed. The flying powder turned our hair to white. And all the time we'd chat like squirrels or sing so full of mirth that if some stranger happened by, he'd never guess we toiled to hollow out a place where one of us would shortly lie.

Reginald would shake his head and chide.

"For sure, Father," he'd say, "it is not seemly thus. Durham's full of monks who'd deem this task an honor. Or if you choose to make your grave yourself as Jesu hauled his cross up Calvary, there are fitter folk to help you than this popinjay."

Once, as he scolded, Perkin crept behind and wound a vine about his feet so when he made to go, he tripped and sprawled. In courtesy to the robe he wore, I tried to keep a stately face but failed when Perkin climbed a tree and hooted like an owl.

And then the lid. We happened on a slab of rock that Wear had sliced and trimmed it up to size. Then Reginald came to help us put it into place, but just as we were hoisting it, Perkin made us set it down.

"A tomb's like a shirt," he said. "Don't stitch it up until you're sure it's cut to fit. Climb in and see, old man."

Old man is what he calls me to this day, and Reginald always rolls his eyes and groans at it, though as for me, I do not mind. I'm old. I am a man, or was one once. So where's the harm? In any case, I did as I was bade. With one of them beneath each arm, I managed to climb in and lay me down.

"Why look!" cried Perkin. "See, there's room enough for two!" and quick as a wink he clambered in and stretched himself the other way from me. His toe just missed my eye. We didn't tarry long, but while we did, I watched the sky and thought how when my time comes round to lie there till the angel sounds his horn, my tomb will seem less lonely far for knowing that my boy once lay there too.

When I was Perkin's age, I could not write my name, but by that time I'd learned, and thus we carved the letters in that set together in a row spell Godric out. Perkin said there should be something more and with a white stone scratched a likeness of my face, but years of rain have long since washed it out. It was no loss. The face was mostly nose and beard and looked more like a lobster than a man.

He also said we should carve in the year and place where I was born, but I said no. As a man dies many times before he's dead, so does he wend from birth to birth until, by grace, he comes alive at last. Not Wear but far away another river saw the birth of me that mattered most, and the year was the year that Deric died and Godric swam away from Mouse and first set foot upon the holy shore.

Of Jerusalem and what befell Godric there.

DEAR Jesu, teach me how to pray. I know but little Latin like the priests. Except for Baldwin, I've never spoken to a king apart from thee. I've never learned to wrap my tongue round courtly talk. The only words I know are words of earth and wood and stone fit best for rough, unlettered folk like me. When people come to gawk at me, or Reginald comes, or Durham monks, the air is so a-buzz with words that, when they go, I sometimes do not speak for days. I use my hands instead. One finger set upon my lips means food, and two mean drink. A wagging back and forth before my eyes means go. A single hand outstretched means come. Dear Lord, were I in such a wise to pray, I'd have to have a spider's limbs for hands enough to stretch my need to thee.

What can I tell thee thou dost not already know? What can I ask of thee thou wilt not give unasked if that's thy will? Yet I must ask thee even so. The time I saw Jerusalem, for one. With all that lies upon thy heart, dost thou remember that? Didst thou, who saidst, God's eye is on the sparrow, cast thine eye on me? A friar with a cross led me and other palmers to the sites where thou didst cruelly suffer here on earth. At each we stopped and knelt. And every time we did, I felt thy presence near as breath. Oh wert thou near in truth, or was it only that I wished it so?

The friar took us to the court where Pilate had thee flogged and showed us traces of thy blood and fingerprints upon the stone. Then didst thou hear me as I called thy name? Didst mark the tears that trickled down my beard? Oh dost thou hear and mark me now, sweet King? Old Godric has to hope that hope or else his heart, which by thy grace has thumped these hundred years, must crack at last. Amen.

Jerusalem flashed awesome in the sun when I came from Jaffa that first day on foot. She was spread upon the hills, her white walls marked with trees and shrubbery that dived to valleys dark and deep. Her rocky slopes were strewn with olive groves, her domes and towers painted gold and blue. Her roofs were rose and white and green. She was so fair I saw at once how men could die for her as Franks and Turks are dying still, God knows. Still battered from my fight with Mouse, I entered through her gates as in a dream. If so, it was a dream of thee.

How different she was from Rome. Rome was the sights you paid a crook-back guide to show. Rome was the broken bones of ancient times. Rome was goats and owls where once great Caesar's palace stood. Even the holiness of Rome was of another age, for all that passes now for holy there seems dim beside the Rome where Paul and Peter bled. Rome was a city men had built and other men had razed and burned. Jerusalem is God's.

When thou earnest riding in upon an ass and the folk all welcomed thee with shouts of praise and palms, thou saidst if they were still, the very stones would cry aloud instead. And so they do. The streets. The walls. The earth itself. All cries. Rome and her glory were of all things dead. Jerusalem is still alive with thee.

I was the most alone I've ever been. I'd left the *Saint Esprit* and Mouse for good. Deric was no more. Home was a thousand miles away. Of all the pilgrims, knights, and infidels that thronged the streets, there was not even one I knew. Like a snail that hauls his shell upon his back, I carried all I was on mine. And how life loads us down!

Burcwen's bitterness and William's humble kissing of my hand the dawn I left as if he thought he was not worthy even to be called his brother's friend. The lady Hedwic weeping in the night. The cat whose throat I'd slit for martyr's blood in Bishop's Lynn. Poor weaver Small who might be weaving still had I not found him crouched behind that tomb and made him stand to catch the Yorkshire cobblers' murderous eyes. The poor I'd cropped to make them sprout for Baron Falkes, the ones I'd pirated with Mouse. There was no cruel nor witless wrong I ever worked that didn't weigh me down.

And add to that the good I might have done but shirked. Old Cherryman, the priest, who groaned all night remembering his fallen sons. How painless had it been to speak some word of comfort in the dark that might have eased his pain a bit. The wife with child who swung upon her husband's feet. I might have somehow succored her. And all the beggars that I saw in Rome and everywhere, the rack-ribbed children and the blind, the lepers with their loathsome sores. How could I bury treasure deep on Farne that might have bought for each a pennysworth of hope?

Dear Christ, have mercy on my soul. And Aedlward, have mercy too. I've chided you for failing as a father, too spent from grubbing to have any love to spend on me. Maybe it was the other way around, and it was I that failed you as a son: Did I ever bring you broth? Was any word I ever spoke a word to cheer your weariness? All this, and more than this, I bore upon my back from holy place to holy place.

I saw the spot Our Lady met thee carrying thy cross. She swooned and fell. I saw where thou didst wash the dusty feet of those who, when the soldiers came to haul thee off to death, took to their well-washed heels. With a candle in my hand I climbed the hill on which they nailed thee to a tree, thy tender flesh so rent and torn it was more full of wounds than ever was a dovehouse full of holes. In a round-shaped church of stone where knights kept vigil, I saw thy Holy Sepulchre itself, the very shelf they set thy body on. How dark those three days must have been that thou didst lie in death, nor any savior at God's throne to plead man's cause! I kissed a piece of that same stone the angel rolled away to set thee free, and at another church they'd built where thou didst rise to God, I kissed thy footprints in the rock and through an opening in the roof beheld the very channel in the sky that thou didst sail to Paradise.

Then I tramped to the river Jordan where the Baptist baptised thee. A chapel stood on stilts to mark the spot. They were singing mass inside. The voices sounded faraway and soft. Dusk fell. A rope was stretched from bank to bank to help the cripples in who came to bathe in hope the water thou hadst cleansed as it cleansed thee would make their bent limbs straight again.

A long-necked bird with spindle legs picked through the rushes at the river's edge. There was no one there but him and me and, dimly seen above, the evening star. I stood and watched the Jordan flow a while, not rough like Wear but flat and still. Then waded in.

Oh Lord, the coolness of the river's touch! The way it mirrored back the clouds as if I bathed in sky. I waded out to where the water reached my neck, my beard outspread, my garments floating free. I let my hands bob up like corks. At sixteen stone or more, I felt I had, myself, no weight at all. The soul, set free from flesh at last, must know such peace.

And oh, the heart, the heart! In Jordan to my chin, I knew not if I laughed or wept but only that the untold weight of sin upon my heart was gone. I ducked my head beneath, and in the dark I thought I heard that porpoise voice again that spoke to me the day I nearly drowned in Wash. "Take, eat me, Godric, to thy soul's delight. Hold fast to him who gave his life for thee and thine." When I came up again, I cried like one gone daft for joy.

"Be fools for Christ," said the Apostle Paul, and thus I was thy bearded Saxon fool and clown for sure. Nothing I ever knew before and nothing I have ever come to know from then till now can match the holy mirth and madness of that time. Many's the sin I've clipped to since. Many's the dark and savage night of doubt. Many's the prayer I haven't prayed, the friend I've hurt, the kindness left undone. But this I know. The Godric that waded out of Jordan soaked and dripping wet that day was not the Godric that went wading in.

O Thou that asketh much of him to whom thou givest much, have mercy. Remember me not for the ill I've done but for the good I've dreamed. Help me to be not just the old and foolish one thou seest now but once again a fool for thee. Help me to pray. Help me whatever way thou canst, dear Christ and Lord. Amen.

*How Godric filled his time, and certain
holy sights he saw.*

I'VE lived at Finchale fifty years, and thus my near a hundred, give or take, are split in two, The first half teems with places that I saw and deeds I did and folk I knew. The second half I've dwelled here by myself. Three times only have I left, such as the day I went to Christmas Mass at Durham. Except for those the monks give plaited crosses to, I've scarcely seen a living soul apart from Reginald, and Ailred now and then, and Perkin, God be praised. The lad is twenty-some and started bringing eggs to me when he himself was little bigger than an egg. So, by the reckoning of men, one half my life has been an empty box. Yet if they only understood, it's been the fuller of the two. Three things I've filled it with: *what used to be, what might have been,* and, for the third, *what may be yet* and in some measure *is* already had we only eyes to see.

Voices that I haven't heard since I was young call out to me. Faces long since faded bloom afresh. Legs that barely hold me up grow strong again in dreams to carry me wherever I would go and where I wouldn't too.

"That hermit Godric!" people say. "How holy must he be to rest in one place, rooted like a tree, so he may raise his shaggy arms to God alone while holy thoughts nest in his leaves like birds."

They do not guess that in my mind I'm never still. Seven times seven are the seas I've sailed in less times than it takes to tell. I can draw my breath on Dover Road and puff it out again in Rome. And oh the thoughts that come to roost in this old skull!

When I'm awake, I'm master of them well enough. Let some woman that I lay with once come chirping lechery in my memory's ear, I've but to clap my hands and she will usually fly away. Or let some ancient grievance croak, some long forgotten hunger whet his beak for more, some foolish pride start preening in the sun, and I've such arms as these old pot-lids that I wear for vest, or icy Wear, or holy prayer, to fend them off. But hermits sleep like other men, alas, and in the dark all men go mad.

Oh what a crop of sons the seed I've spilled in dreams would raise! How many silken coverlets I'd need to cover all the naked flesh I've dallied with in lust though lying all alone the while in rags with calluses thick as cobbles on my knees from prayer. Sometimes maids whom, in the daylight world, I held in such esteem I wouldn't have so much as thought to kiss them save in greeting or farewell, in sleep I've sported with so shamelessly that when I waked, I wept to think on what I'd done. Even to the priest who comes to shrive me now and then, I can't bring myself to name their names. Dear Lord, strew herbs upon my hermit's dreams to make them sweet. Have daylight mercy on my midnight soul.

After such fashion I fill the box of empty years with thinking back on how things were—some good, some bad—and dreaming into life again what's dead and gone. The things that might have been have less in them of sin, perhaps, and yet they're still sadder in their way. An old man's thoughts are long. He falters back to all the crossroads of the years and wonders how he would have fared if he'd gone right instead of left.

Suppose I'd not strung Burcwen from a branch that day but taken her along? Suppose some other man than Mouse had ferried me to Farne? What if I'd stayed with Falkes de Granvill and grown rich? Where would I be if Gillian hadn't left me in the wood, or if I'd taken me a wife and settled down? Our children's children's children now might be the ones to bring me eggs and comb the cobwebs from my beard. Say Mouse and I had never fought. Say Aedlward had lived to be not just my father but my friend.

Was it God who led me on the way I went, or was his will that I should take some different turn? Life's a list. Good tilts with ill. The de Granvills of the world grow fat. Poor folk eat earth. Even in his church, the Lord is mocked by lustful, greedy monks and priests that steal. Men travel leagues to see the arm of some dead martyr in a silver sleeve that wouldn't lift a hand to save a living child that's fallen in a well. King wars with Pope, and mighty lords attack the King. Bishops like Flambard are but mighty lords themselves with crosses hung about their necks. When Stephen and Matilda strove together for the crown not long ago, the land went lawless. Castles were filled with fiends that burned and tore and flayed men's flesh for gold while God and all his angels seemed to sleep.

All that is out where men can see. Inside, the same old woes go on. Folk lie sick with none to nurse them. Good men die before their time. Their wives and children weep with none to care. The old go daft with loneliness. The young turn sour. Faith's forsaken. Hope takes wing. And charity, the greatest of the three, is scarce as water in a drought.

And what has Godric done for God or fellowmen through all of this? Godric's war is all within. For fifty years the only foe he's battled with has been himself. Above all else, he's prayed.

What's prayer? It's shooting shafts into the dark. What mark they strike, if any, who's to say? It's reaching for a hand you cannot touch. The silence is so fathomless that prayers like plummets vanish in the sea. You beg. You whimper. You load God down with empty praise. You tell him sins that he already knows full well. You seek to change his changeless will. Yet Godric prays the way he breathes, for else his heart would wither in his breast. Prayer is the wind that fills his sail. Else waves would dash him on the rocks, or he would drift with witless tides. And sometimes, by God's grace, a prayer is heard.

Once I knelt outside my cell at dawn. A mist from Wear had hung the leaves with pearls. I'd scattered ashes on my head. For days I'd eaten nothing but a broth of wild angelica that Elric said kept demons off. "Fair Queen of Heaven," I prayed, "God's turned his back on us for sin. The world is dark. Oh thou, his lady mother, take our cause. Beseech him to forget his wrath. Thou knowest from thy days on earth how hard it is to be a man. If thou wilt only kneel before his throne, he must again be merciful for sure. Hail Mary, Mother, pray for us."

I raised my eyes. A lady all in sky-blue mist stood nigh. She wore a golden crown. Her eyes were pearls. Her voice was like clear water in a brook. And then it was she taught her song to me. Its last words were *Our Lady, maiden, springtime's flower, deliver Godric from this hour.* "Deliver everyone of us!" I cried. "Deliver all who call on thee!" Her face grew soft with holy mirth. She bowed her head most graciously and smiled. Then she was gone.

Another time I lay awake at night. Tune was sleeping in his jar. The moon was full. "Lord God," I prayed. "How useless is my life. My flesh is ever prey to lust and pride and sloth. I let folk call me Holy Father though I know myself to be of all God's sinful sons most foul. Even as I speak to thee, a thousand wanton dreams are set to fall on me when I am done. Oh send some saint to save my soul. Teach me how to serve thee right."

Then all at once a shaft of moonlight clove my cell, and in it stood the body of a man. By the leather girdle round his waist, I knew him for the Baptist. He cried, "Burn! Burn! Serve man and God as fire does by driving back the night. Let thy very rage against thy sin burst into flame. Dwell here alone and by hot striving to be pure become a torch to light men's way and scorch the wings of fiends. Seek not saints to ease thy spirit's pain that thou mayst better serve. Thy pain's itself thy service. Godric, burn for God!"

Tune raised his head and hissed. A cloud passed by the hazy moon, and all was black.

One summer day I lay upon the grass. I'd sinned, no matter how, and in sin's wake there came a kind of drowsy peace so deep I hadn't even will enough to loathe myself. I had no mind to pray. I scarcely had a mind at all, just eyes to see the greenwood overhead, just flesh to feel the sun.

A light breeze blew from Wear that tossed the trees, and as I lay there watching them, they formed a face of shadows and of leaves. It was a man's green, leafy face. He gazed at me from high above. And as the branches nodded in the air, he opened up his mouth to speak. No sound came from his lips, but by their shape I knew it was my name.

His was the holiest face I ever saw. My very name turned holy on his tongue. If he had bade me rise and follow to the end of time, I would have gone. If he had bade me die for him, I would have died. When I deserved it least, God gave me most. I think it was the Savior's face itself I saw.

About Us

Frederick Buechner (pronounced BEEK-ner) (http://en.wikipedia.org/wiki/Frederick_Buechner) is an American writer and theologian. He is the author of more than thirty published books and has been an important source of inspiration and learning for many readers. His work encompasses many genres, including fiction, autobiography, essays, sermons, and other nonfiction. Buechner's books have been translated into 27 languages for publication around the world. Buechner's writing has often been praised for its ability to inspire readers to see the grace in their daily lives.

Buechner has been called "major talent" by the New York Times, and "one of our most original storytellers" by USA Today. Annie Dillard (Pulitzer Prize-winning author of *Pilgrim at Tinker Creek*) says: "Frederick Buechner is one of our finest writers." As stated in the London Free Press, "He is one of our great novelists because he is one of our finest religious writers." He has been a finalist for the Pulitzer Prize and the National Book Award, and has been awarded eight honorary degrees from such institutions as Yale University and the Virginia Theological Seminary. In addition, Buechner has been the recipient of the O. Henry Award, the Rosenthal Award, the Christianity and

Literature Belles Lettres Prize, and has been recognized by the American Academy and Institute of Arts and Letters.

The Frederick Buechner Center (www.frederickbuechner.com) was established to share the works of Christian author Frederick Buechner with communities around the world. All after-tax net profits of the Frederick Buechner Center website are donated for educational and charitable purposes.

Anne Lamott (www.facebook.com/AnneLamott) is an American novelist and non-fiction writer. She is also a progressive political activist and public speaker. Based in the San Francisco Bay Area, her non-fiction works are largely autobiographical. Marked by their self-deprecating humor and openness, Lamott's writings cover such subjects as alcoholism, single-motherhood, depression, and Christianity.

Brian D. McLaren (www.brianmclaren.net) is an author, speaker, activist, and public theologian. A former college English teacher and pastor, he is an ecumenical global networker among innovative Christian leaders.

Barbara Brown Taylor (www.barbarabrowntaylor.com) is the Butman Professor of Religion at Piedmont College in rural northeast Georgia. An Episcopal priest since 1984, she is the author of thirteen books, including the New York Times bestsellers *Learning to Walk in the Dark* and *An Altar in the World*. Her first memoir, *Leaving Church*, won a 2006 Author of the Year award from the Georgia Writers Association.

W. Dale Brown, the founding director of the Buechner Speaker Series at King University, was the author of numerous articles and the critical biography, *The Book of Buechner: A Journey Through His Writings.* For twenty years, Brown was a professor of English at Calvin College in Grand Rapids, Michigan and for more than ten years was the director of the Festival of Faith & Writing there. A frequent speaker at academic conferences and churches, Brown taught literature and journalism courses at King University, where he chaired the English department.